Kidspiration® in the Classroom

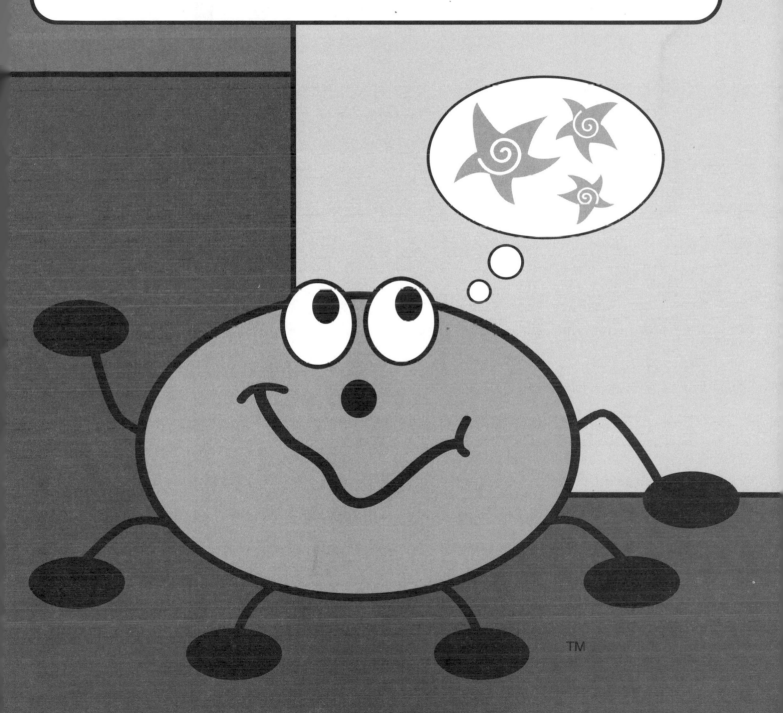

Inspiration®
SOFTWARE, INC

7412 SW Beaverton Hillsdale Hwy, Ste. 102, Portland, OR 97225-2167 USA
Phone 503-297-3004   Fax 503-297-4676   www.inspiration.com

Publisher: Mona L. Westhaver

Authors: Mary Chase, Ph.D. and Bob Madar

Editor: Jonathan Maier

Associate Editor: Linnea Johnsson

Layout/Design: Christine Washburn

Kidspiration in the Classroom

Introduction

Learning to think. Learning to learn. These are the essential skills for student success. Scientifically based research and educational theory tell us that visual learning techniques—graphical ways of working with ideas—are among the best methods for teaching students how to think and how to learn. The use of graphic organizers helps students develop important comprehension, thinking and writing skills.

Kidspiration® in the Classroom supports the development of these important skills. It provides practical guidance for implementing Kidspiration and visual learning across the curriculum to improve achievement. The lessons in this book are based on standards derived from individual states and professional organizations. For those educators new to Kidspiration, the activities will make it easy to get started quickly. Veteran users will discover new applications and trainers will find ways to customize workshops.

At Inspiration Software®, Inc. our mission is to make a positive difference in students' lives. We are committed to providing innovative tools that inspire students and help them build key "learning to learn" skills. We hope the strategies presented here will serve your students throughout their education and provide a foundation for lifelong learning.

Mona L. Westhaver

Mona L. Westhaver
Co-founder and President
Inspiration Software, Inc.

About Kidspiration® in the Classroom

 ## Organization

The main sections of *Kidspiration® in The Classroom* reflect the four major curriculum areas: Reading and Writing, Social Studies, Science and Math. Within each section, lessons are designated grades K-2 or 3-5. You may find it helpful to review lessons from grade levels outside your area; many lessons can easily be modified for other content and classrooms. Additional sections at the end of the book offer further resources for curriculum development and enrichment.

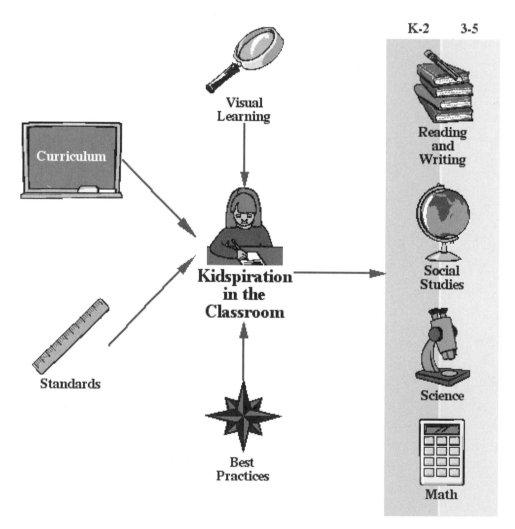

iv

Downloadable activities and examples

Many of the Kidspiration activities and examples found throughout this book were designed specifically for these lessons. These valuable and time-saving resources are easily downloaded at www.inspiration.com/kitc. Please note: If an activity is mentioned without reference to downloading, then it is already available in Kidspiration.

Get inspired!

We hope this book inspires you to make the lessons your own: mold them to match your teaching style and the needs of your students. Feel free to contact us with your questions, insights and great ideas. We love to hear from educators!

v

Table of Contents

Reading and Writing

Social Studies

Science

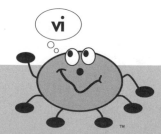

Kidspiration in the Classroom

Table of Contents

Kidspiration in the Classroom

Reading and Writing

Sight Word Rebuses

✺ Overview

Acquiring a sight word vocabulary leads to reading fluency. In this lesson, students work with words from the Dolch Sight Word List and Fry's 300 Instant Sight Words to strengthen their sentence building skills.

✺ Standard

Students recognize and understand grade level sight words and high frequency words.

✺ Preparation

Download the Sight Word activity at www.inspiration.com/kitc or refer to the How To section, page 102, to create your own version.

Note: In this activity, some text is written in white so students can use the Listen tool to hear word order without seeing the words.

✺ Lesson

1. Open the Sight Word activity and model its use for students. Demonstrate how to hear the target sentences by turning on the Listen tool and clicking on the symbol labeled "Listen." Show how to reorder the words and symbols in the corresponding SuperGrouper® rectangle to duplicate the sentence.

2. Instruct students to work individually on the activity. Circulate among students to review their work, noting problems and misunderstandings.

3. Have students form small teams and open a new Kidspiration® document. Direct them to add several symbols and take turns entering words they know from their reading books into the symbols. Encourage teams to include picture symbols of their choice. To show symbol labels, instruct teams to click twice on the Hide/Show Captions button on the Formatting toolbar.

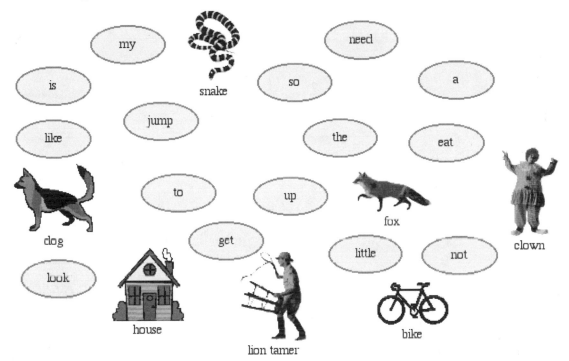

4. Challenge teams to link their words and symbols to create rebus sentences. Encourage them to create new symbols and words if needed. Remind them to capitalize and enter punctuation and verb endings.

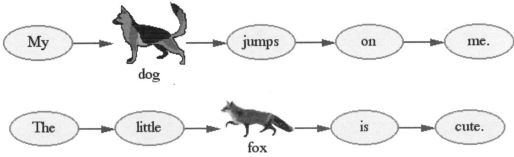

Reading and Writing | Grades K-2

Describe It!

 Overview

Parts of speech can be difficult to understand when studied formally. In this lesson, students use pictures and writing to explore the use of adjectives in context.

 Standards

• Students learn parts of speech and grammatical conventions.

• Students use adjectives to produce descriptive writing.

 Preparation

1. Download the What Kind activity at www.inspiration.com/kitc or refer to the How To section, page 102, to create your own version.

What kind of apple?

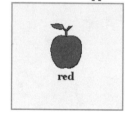

red

What kind of ostrich?

What kind of soup?

2. Open the Reading and Writing—Adjectives activity and modify it to correspond with your students' developmental levels (for example, reduce the number of adjective symbols). Refer to the How To section, page 102, to save the modified version as an activity.

What kind of face?

What kind of pig?

What kind of character?

3. Prior to the lesson, share stories with your class that use descriptive adjectives (for example, *Ten, Nine, Eight* by Molly Bang or *Swimmy* by Leo Lionni).

 Lesson

1. Discuss descriptive words with students, and use examples from recent reading. Point out that descriptive words answer the question, "What kind?"

2. Open the What Kind activity and demonstrate its use. Talk through the process as you select a symbol and enter an adjective.

Kidspiration in the Classroom

3. Divide students into pairs and ask them to open the What Kind activity. Instruct them to label each symbol with an appropriate adjective. Circulate and point out interesting word choices. Check for comprehension.

4. Have students remain in pairs and open the Adjectives activity you modified earlier. Instruct them to choose one symbol to describe by entering adjectives into the associated symbols.

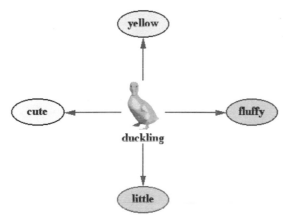

 Extension

Encourage students to use the Symbol Maker stamps to create symbols that illustrate a scene. Have students challenge other students to write or record a descriptive sentence about the symbols.

The <u>happy</u> cat has the <u>dog's</u> bone.

A <u>little</u> bunny is in the <u>cold</u> snow.

The <u>blue</u> cat has a <u>red</u> hat.

Here is a <u>little red</u> fish and a <u>big blue</u> fish.

13

Pattern Books

 Overview

One of the most important ways to help emerging readers and writers develop their literacy skills is by exposing them to literature that makes use of structural patterns. In this lesson, students build an awareness of story patterns and write their own version of a pattern book.

 Standards

• Students read a range of print materials to build an understanding of text.

• Students recognize patterns in familiar stories and poems.

• Students use semantic and syntactic cues to aid comprehension and make predictions about content.

 Preparation

1. Download the Brown Bear activity at www.inspiration.com/kitc or refer to the How To section, page 102, to create your own version.

2. Prior to the lesson, allow students to choose symbols from the People symbol libraries to represent themselves or use the Symbol Maker to create self-portraits. Install these in a custom library (refer to the How To section, page 104).

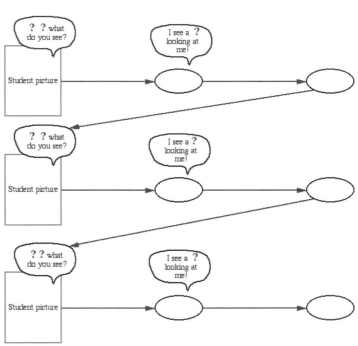

 Lesson

1. Read aloud *Brown Bear, Brown Bear, What Do You See?*, by Bill Martin, Jr. As students begin to recognize the book's pattern and predict what will come next, encourage them to "read" along with you.

2. Tell students they will be creating a class story based on the Brown Bear book. Open the Brown Bear activity and ask for a volunteer to go first. Select the first symbol and replace it with the appropriate symbol from the custom library you created earlier. Label it with the student's name.

14

3. Have the student volunteer choose an animal from the Animals symbol libraries to start a new book. Replace the second symbol with the chosen animal. Read the first talking bubble symbol, and ask students what word should replace each question mark. Enter the name of the animal and use the Listen tool to hear the sentence read.

4. To personalize the activity further, suggest the volunteer use the Record tool to add his or her own voice to the activity.

5. Continue through the class, inviting each student to add to the story.

6. The next day, review *Brown Bear, Brown Bear, What Do You See?* with students, and ask which of the five senses the book uses as part of the pattern. Ask how they might use the other senses to create a similar pattern book. For example, "Black cat, black cat what do you hear? I hear a _____ drawing near."

7. Divide the class into teams, and instruct them to work together to create a pattern book that uses a different sense.

✦ Extension

Challenge students to create a diagram based on other pattern books or poems, such as "This is the House that Jack Built."

Reading and Writing | Grades K-2

Using Story Cues

 ## Overview

One of the primary strategies in reading comprehension is prediction. In this lesson, students explore predictive elements and use them to analyze stories.

 ## Standards

• Students recognize sequence, setting, characters, main events and plot in stories.

• Students acquire a variety of strategies for predicting content and meaning.

 ## Preparation

1. Review the Reading and Writing—Story Web activity and, if necessary, modify it to reflect your students' reading levels. Refer to the How To section, page 102, to save the modified activity.

2. Gather a collection of books with recognizable predictive elements and encourage students to look through the books during free time.

3. During the week prior to the lesson, allow students to choose books from the collection for you to read aloud. As you read, pause at appropriate spots and ask students what they think will happen next and how they know.

4. Choose two stories that use the same predictive element (for example, disobedience, as presented in traditional versions of "Little Red Riding Hood" and Tomie de Paola's *Strega Nona*) to model the Story Web activity.

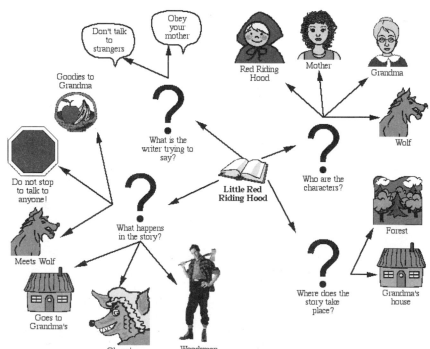

16

Lesson

1. Read aloud one of the stories you chose earlier. Open the Story Web activity and model it using information from the story you just read.

2. The next day, review the Story Web activity. Tell students they will be completing the activity for the next story you will read, so they should listen carefully.

3. Read the story and check for comments and questions.

4. Divide the class into small teams and instruct them to open the Story Web activity. Ask them to use it to explore the story you just read. Remind them they can use the Symbol Maker tool and the Record command to help them express their ideas. Make the book available to teams for reference.

5. Assist teams as they create their diagrams, clarifying any misunderstandings.

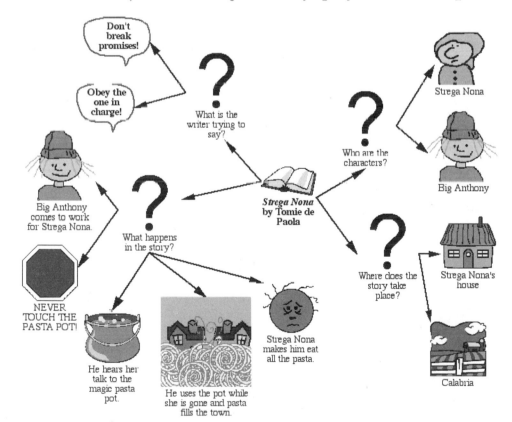

6. Print the team diagrams and post them so students can see the variety of responses. Discuss similarities and differences with the class.

(17)

Creating a Glossary

 ## Overview

Students are more likely to recall information when they organize and represent the ideas themselves. In this lesson, students use images and their own words to create a personal glossary for a unit on mythology.

 ## Standards

• Students identify and organize key words from a unit of study.

• Students use details to clarify and enhance meaning.

• Students know common roots and affixes derived from Greek and Latin, and use this knowledge to analyze the meaning of complex words.

 ## Preparation

1. Download the following Glossary activity at www.inspiration.com/kitc or refer to the How To section, page 102, to create your own version.

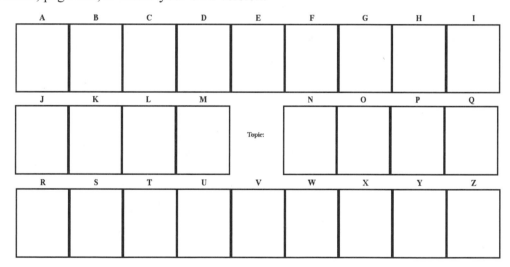

2. Gather informational materials on Greek and Roman mythology.

 ## Lesson

1. Allow students time to peruse the informational materials on Greek and Roman mythology. Instruct them to make note of new words and names as they encounter them.

2. Open the Glossary activity and enter the topic of study into the appropriate symbol.

3. Review the activity with students, and tell them they will be adding their new words to the chart in order to create a personal glossary. Demonstrate entering new words.

Kidspiration in the Classroom

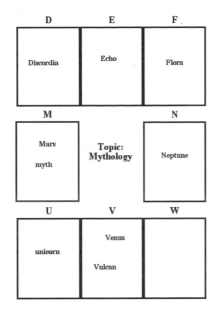

D	E	F
Discordia	Echo	Flora

M		N
Mars myth	Topic: Mythology	Neptune

U	V	W
unicorn	Venus Vulcan	

4. Replace some of the words with symbols, and discuss the use of pictures as memory cues.

5. Make the activity available to students, and have them maintain it during the unit, adding new words and concepts as they arise.

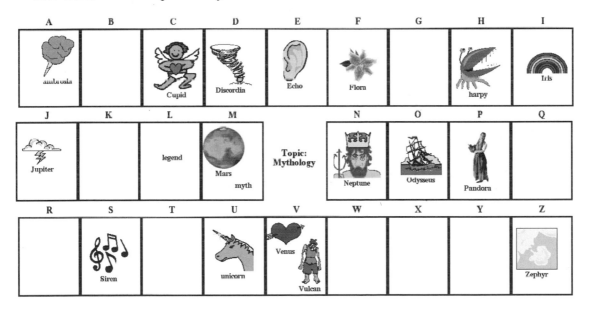

A	B	C	D	E	F	G	H	I
ambrosia		Cupid	Discordia	Echo	Flora		harpy	Iris

J	K	L	M		N	O	P	Q
Jupiter		legend	Mars myth	Topic: Mythology	Neptune	Odysseus	Pandora	

R	S	T	U	V	W	X	Y	Z
	Siren		unicorn	Venus Vulcan				Zephyr

6. Encourage students to switch to Writing View to add descriptions, examples and other notes.

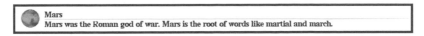

Mars
Mars was the Roman god of war. Mars is the root of words like martial and march.

7. Call on students to share their entries with the rest of the class on a regular basis. Remind them to use the glossary as a study tool.

Reading and Writing | Grades 3-5

Reading Reflection

 Overview

Encouraging free reading of self-selected books is a valuable classroom practice. In this lesson, students use their free reading books as sources for reflection and analysis.

 Standards

- Students use a variety of methods to make, confirm and revise predictions during the reading process.

- Students use reading strategies to understand a variety of texts.

- Students understand basic elements of plot and character development in literary works.

 Preparation

Download the Reading Journal activity at www.inspiration.com/kitc or refer to the How To section, page 102, to create your own version.

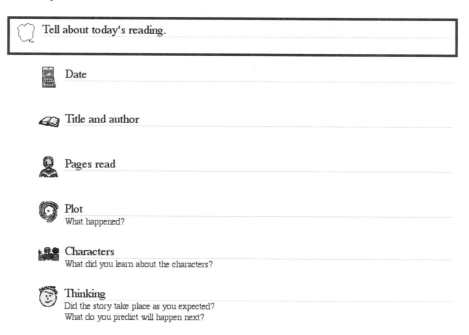

 Lesson

1. Open the Reading Journal activity and model its use for students. Record information from a book with which students are familiar.

2. Invite students to contribute ideas and enter them into the activity.

3. Have students open the Reading Journal activity after each free reading period and record their thoughts.

20

Date
October 7

 Title and author
The Littles by John Peterson

 Pages read
20-22

 Plot
What happened? The Newcombs are very messy and do not throw away garbage. Granny thinks mice will come!

 Characters
What did you learn about the characters? Lucy is always scared.

 Thinking
Did the story take place as you expected? I thought from the picture that a cat would come but so far there's no cat.
What do you predict will happen next? I think Granny is right. Maybe a cat will come to catch the mice.

4. Instruct students to print their Reading Journal to maintain an ongoing reading log. Have them share the log on a regular basis with their reading group.

5. When students finish reading a book, instruct them to review their logs and open a new Kidspiration® document in Picture View. Have them use symbols and links to show the flow of story events. Encourage them to use words that denote sequence (for example, then, so and next) as link text.

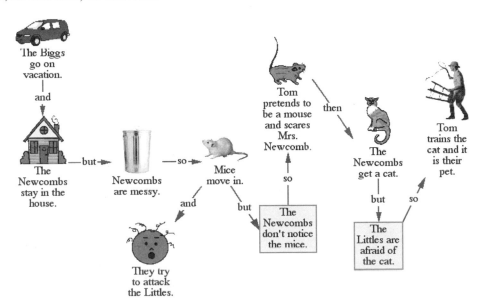

6. Use students' flow diagrams to discuss event sequences, character interactions and cause-effect relationships.

Writing for an Audience

Overview

Students write at a level somewhat lower than their reading level, so younger children are a perfect audience for their compositions. In this lesson, students plan and write a report on a subject that interests younger students and share it with them.

Standards

• Students use a variety of strategies to identify topics to investigate.

• Students use a variety of print and non-print sources to gather information.

• Students use strategies to gather and record research information.

• Students use strategies to write for different audiences.

Preparation

1. Arrange for a primary class to partner with your students. Make sure there is sufficient age range between the groups. For example, partner a third grade class with kindergartners rather than a second grade class.

2. Ask the partner teacher to have his or her students brainstorm topics they want to know more about.

Lesson

1. Inform students they will be writing reports for children at the primary level. Have students select a topic to explore from among those brainstormed by the primary grade audience.

2. Tell students to identify at least eight facts about their topic and take notes on their findings. Assist students as they use the library or Internet to research.

3. Have students open the More—Five Facts activity. Discuss what makes one fact more important than another and what facts their will understand. Tell students to identify five good facts from their research notes and enter them into the appropriate symbols. Encourage them to add subtopics as necessary.

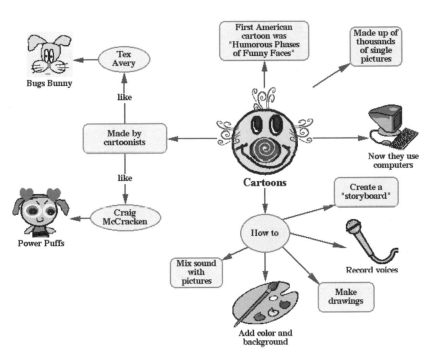

4. Have students switch to Writing View to add further detail.

> • **First American cartoon was "Humorous Phases of Funny Faces"**
> This was a black and white movie of a guy's hand drawing funny faces.

• **Made up of thousands of single pictures**
When they show all these pictures one after the other, it looks like the pictures are moving.

• **Now they use computers**
They use the computer to copy the same picture over and over so they don't have to draw it more than once. Now even kids can make cartoons on a computer.

5. Discuss the reading level of the target audience with students. Ask students to make sure they are using clear, simple vocabulary, and suggest dividing longer sentences into shorter ones. Have students use the Listen tool to check for awkward construction or other problems they may have missed when reading silently.

6. Before students publish their report, remind them the diagram in Picture View will serve as the illustration for their report. Encourage them to return to Picture View to add symbols. If necessary, have them rearrange their diagram for clarity.

7. From Writing View, have students click the Publish button to finalize their report in a word processor.

8. If possible, take your class to visit the partner classroom and share their reports with small groups interested in their topics. Encourage them to ask their audience for comments, questions and other feedback.

(23)

Poetic Practice

 ## Overview

In this lesson, students combine reading and writing skills to analyze poems and create their own.

 ## Standards

• Students construct meaning using a variety of interpretive strategies.

• Students use reading skills and strategies to understand a variety of literary passages and texts.

• Students write in a variety of genres.

 ## Preparation

1. Download the Write a Poem activity at www.inspiration.com/kitc or refer to the How To section, page 102, to create your own version.

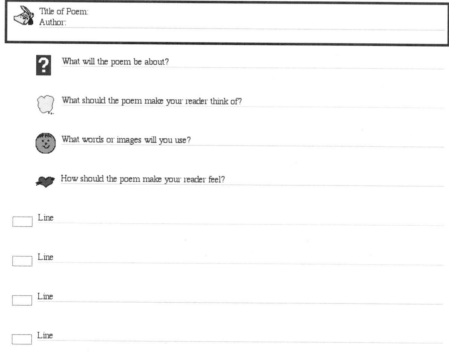

| Title of Poem: |
| Author: |

? What will the poem be about?

What should the poem make your reader think of?

What words or images will you use?

How should the poem make your reader feel?

Line

Line

Line

Line

2. Gather a collection of poetry books and anthologies.

3. During the week before the lesson, read poetry to the class each day and discuss it informally. Be sure to emphasize poetic language and point out lines in which the poet hints at an idea rather than stating it directly. If the class develops favorite poems among those you read, make note of them.

Kidspiration in the Classroom

Lesson

1. Introduce the Reading and Writing—Thinking About Poetry activity. Read one of the class's favorite poems, and ask volunteers to respond to the questions in the activity. Note: For younger students, you may wish to switch to Picture View.

2. Talk through each section of the activity. Point out that sometimes the poem's title is a clue to the meaning, rather than the meaning itself.

3. Have students open the Thinking About Poetry activity. Ask them to use it to analyze a poem they like.

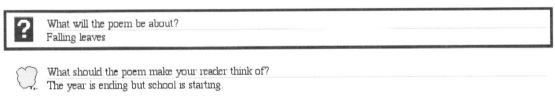

Wind and Silver
by Amy Lowell

What is the poem about?
The moon shines on the water. When the wind blows, the ripples look like dragon scales. It makes the pond sound dangerous.

What did the poem make you think of?
Nature
Magical creatures

What words did you like?
moon
flash
dragon scales

How did the poem make you feel?
I felt excited, but a little scared.

4. Invite students to share their completed activities with others.

5. Open the Write a Poem activity and review it with students. Point out parallels between this activity and the one they just completed.

6. Have students work independently and use the activity to plan a poem.

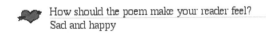 What will the poem be about?
Falling leaves

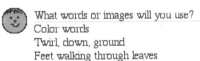 What should the poem make your reader think of?
The year is ending but school is starting.

What words or images will you use?
Color words
Twirl, down, ground
Feet walking through leaves

How should the poem make your reader feel?
Sad and happy

7. Circulate among students to offer suggestions and point out good examples to the rest of the class.

Continued next page

Reading and Writing | Grades 3-5

Poetic Practice

continued

8. Instruct students to begin writing a first draft of their poem. Encourage them to drag and drop topics into new positions, and experiment with different line breaks.

> Red, brown, yellow, orange
>
> Leaves twirl and I twirl through them
>
> We are on our way

9. As students revise, ask them to look for places where their poems could hint at meaning rather than making statements (for example, "calendar pages turn" rather than "time is passing").

10. Instruct students to click the Publish button to finalize their poem in a word processor.

Extension

Have students analyze one another's poems using the Reading and Writing—Thinking About Poetry activity.

Kidspiration in the Classroom

Social Studies

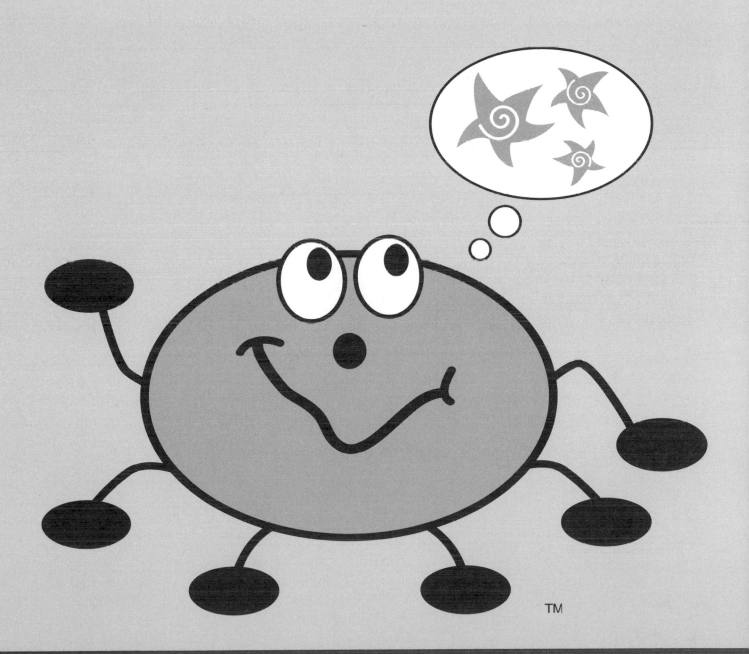

Our Resources

 ## Overview

In this lesson, students gain an appreciation for the resources we get from Earth and think about the consequences of resource depletion.

 ## Standards

• Students know how people depend on the environment.

• Students know the ways resource use affects the environment.

 ## Preparation

1. Download the Our Resources activity at www.inspiration.com/kitc, or refer to the How To section, page 102, to create your own version.

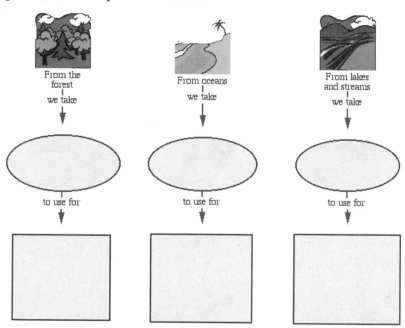

2. Gather informational material on natural resources.

3. Prior to the lesson, encourage students to explore the informational material during free time.

 ## Lesson

1. Open the Our Resources activity and draw students' attention to the Forest symbol.

2. Ask volunteers what resources come from forests. Drag symbols that represent their responses into the appropriate oval SuperGrouper® shape. Enter a label for each symbol and say its name.

Kidspiration in the Classroom

3. Ask students how we use the resources. Drag symbols that represent their responses into the appropriate rectangle SuperGrouper shape. Note that most resources have more than one use.

4. Fill in gaps in student knowledge. For example, students may not know that forests contribute to clean air or that some trees and plants are used to make medicine.

5. Have students open the Our Resources activity and work independently to record additional information about each geographic category. Invite them to consult the informational material on natural resources. Remind them that they can use the Record command to express ideas.

6. Open a new Kidspiration® document. Choose one natural resource you have discussed, and ask students to think about what would happen if the resource were depleted. Record their responses using the Add Symbol tool. Invite volunteers to use the Symbol Maker tool to represent their ideas.

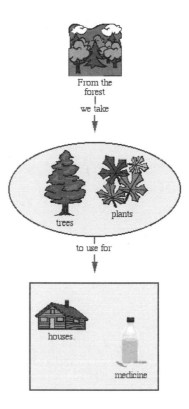

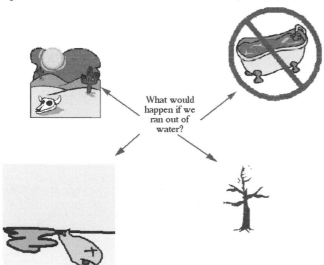

7. Ask students to suggest ways to prevent the disappearance of natural resources.

29

Tools, Talents and Trades

 Overview

In this lesson, students think about different kinds of jobs and skills, and use Kidspiration® to discover how their interests and talents may point the way to a possible career.

 Standards

- Students think about future careers and what they want to accomplish.

- Students relate simple descriptions of work with the names of corresponding jobs.

 Preparation

1. Download the Tools of the Trade and My Tools and Talents activities at www.inspiration.com/kitc or refer to the How To section, page 102, to create your own versions.

2. Gather a collection of books and other resources on careers. Prior to the lesson, encourage students to explore the resources during free time.

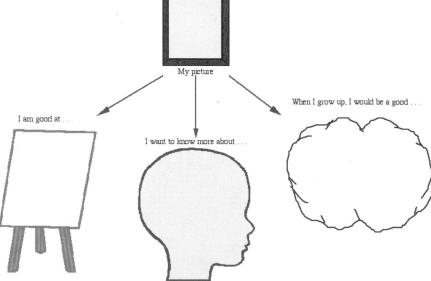

Lesson

1. Distribute the collection of books and other resources on careers among students. Ask students to consult the materials and share examples of jobs and careers.

2. Open the Tools of the Trade activity. Ask students to associate each tool with a job or profession and use their responses to label the appropriate symbols. As you proceed, ask what talents and interests are necessary for each job.

3. Open the My Tools and Talents activity and review it with students. Encourage students to reflect on what they want to do when they grow up, and the tools and talents necessary to reach such a goal.

4. Have students open the My Tools and Talents activity, and use it to record their ideas. Ask them to share it with a friend.

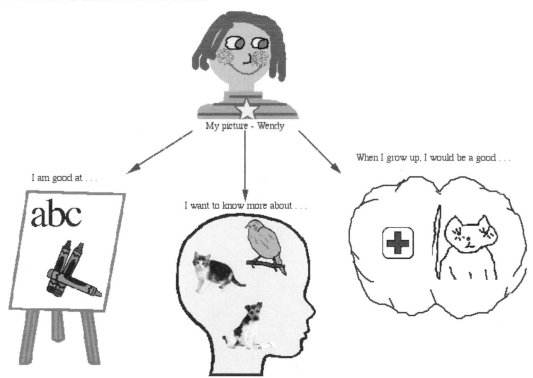

5. Repeat this activity throughout the year. Ask students to compare their new diagrams with those they completed earlier, and discuss the changes they see.

Seasons and Holidays

Overview

Understanding sequence is basic to early learning, and the yearly passage of seasons offers students a familiar example. In this lesson, students use Kidspiration® activities to explore the seasons and connect them to their lives.

Standards

• Students understand the relationship of holidays to traditions and seasons.

• Students recognize sequential relationships and patterns.

Preparation

Download the Which Season activity and A Time For activity at www.inspiration.com/kitc or refer to the How To section, page 102, to create your own versions.

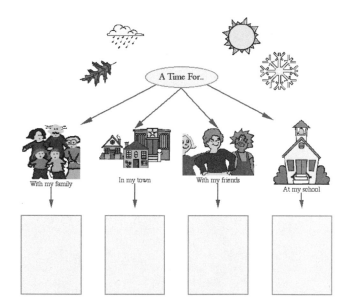

Lesson

1. Have students identify what the current season is. Ask what seasons come next and what they know about each season. Confirm and clarify.

2. Open the Which Season activity. Ask students to identify each of the pictured seasons and explain their thinking. Enter the name of the season into the appropriate label. Spell the season aloud as you type. Repeat, and have students spell with you.

Kidspiration in the Classroom

3. Show students the Holiday symbol libraries and ask volunteers if they see any symbols that suggest specific holidays. Ask the class in which season the holidays occur and drag the symbols into the appropriate season category.

4. Open the A Time For activity, and review it with students. Use your own ideas to model the activity. Demonstrate how to use the Listen tool and Record command to add details.

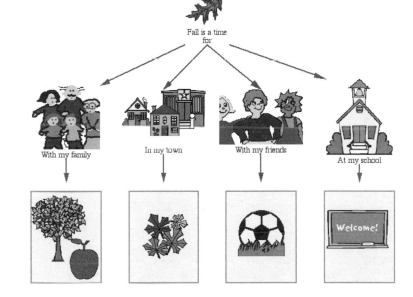

5. Have students open the A Time For activity and assign each student a season to explore. If students cannot find an appropriate symbol, remind them that they can use the Symbol Maker to draw their own symbols.

6. Circulate among students, clarifying and pointing out interesting ideas.

7. Have students form small groups in which each member has explored a different season. Direct students to look for similarities and differences.

 Extension

Invite students to use the More—Venn Diagram activity to compare two seasons, holidays or traditions.

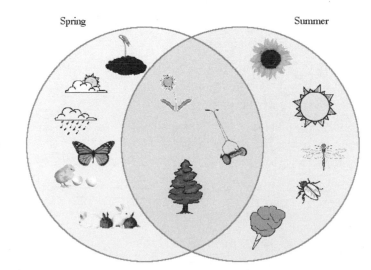

Family Cultures

 ## Overview

Defining similarities among people helps build a sense of community. It is equally important to identify the differences that make us individuals. In this activity, students diagram information about their families, then explore comparisons with other students' families.

 ## Standards

- Students understand similarities and differences among people.

- Students explore family or cultural heritage through stories, songs and celebrations.

- Students know how people share family beliefs and values (for example, oral traditions, literature, songs, art, religion, community celebrations, mementos, food and language).

 ## Preparation

1. Download the About My Family activity at www.inspiration.com/kitc or refer to the How To section, page 102, to create your own version. Note: You may wish to adapt this lesson to accommodate children with non-traditional families or living situations.

2. Open the About My Family activity and switch to Writing View. Print the activity and provide copies to students. For homework, ask them to share the activity with their parents or caregivers and record answers to the listed questions.

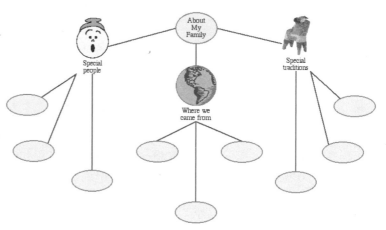

- About My Family
  We are talking about families and what makes them special. Please help your child brainstorm some ideas here. You may wish to use pictures as well as words.

  - Special people
    Who are some special or memorable people in your family?
    - _____

  - Where we came from
    What different states, regions or countries did your family come from?
    - _____

  - Special traditions
    What are some special traditions in your family? (For example, food, celebrations or stories).
    - _____

 **Kidspiration in the Classroom**

Lesson

1. Open the About My Family activity. Tell students about your family and demonstrate how to use the activity by entering your information into the appropriate symbols. Use the Symbol Maker tool at least once to create a symbol, and check for understanding. If your students are emerging writers, show them how to use the Record command to add information.

2. Have students open the About My Family activity. Ask them to consult their homework as they record information about their family. Circulate among students to check for understanding and offer suggestions.

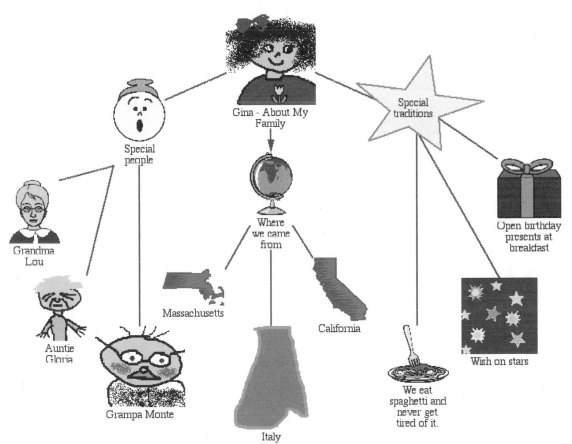

Special people

Grandma Lou

Auntie Gloria

Grampa Monte

Gina - About My Family

Where we came from

Massachusetts

Italy

California

Special traditions

Open birthday presents at breakfast

Wish on stars

We eat spaghetti and never get tired of it.

3. Check student diagrams and look for a category that would offer a good opportunity for comparison. Use this category as the basis of a class discussion on similarities and differences.

State Study

⭐ Overview

Studying the United States of America requires students to manage large amounts of information. In this lesson, students use Kidspiration® to organize and understand facts about states and regions.

⭐ Standard

Students identify various aspects of a state, including location, landforms, bodies of water, climate, economy, population and major cities.

⭐ Preparation

1. Open the Social Studies—State Report activity and modify as below. Name it State Study, and refer to the How To section, page 102, to save it as an activity.

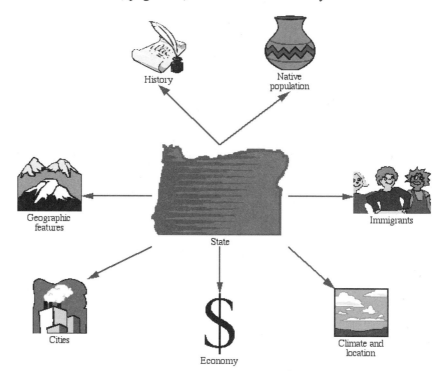

2. Gather a collection of reference materials (for example, atlases and almanacs) and web sites that focus on the states.

⭐ Lesson

1. Open the State Study activity and review the activity's key terms with students. Check for understanding.

Kidspiration in the Classroom

2. Ask students what they already know about the selected state. Help them decide which category their information belongs in and enter their ideas as subtopics.

3. Share the reference materials you gathered and show students how to use almanacs and atlases.

4. Divide the class into teams and assign each team one of the state categories to research.

5. Have each team share what they learned with the rest of the class. Open the State Study activity and switch to Writing View to record their findings.

 Oregon
Motto: *Alis Volat Propiis* "She flies with her own wings"

 History
Oregon was explored by Lewis and Clark.
It became a state in 1859.

 Native population
Oregon tribes are Coos, Grand Ronde, Siletz, Umatilla, Warm Springs, Coquille, Umpqua and Klamath.
The 2000 census lists 45,211 Native Americans in Oregon. There are six reservations.

 Immigrants
At first immigrants came from the Eastern United States and Europe. Later there were Japanese, Vietnamese, Russian, Mexican and many others.

 Climate and location
Bordered by Washington on the north, Idaho on the east, California on the south, Nevada on southeast and the Pacific Ocean on the west.
Very rainy on the western side of the mountains, and dry on the eastern side.

---

6. Assign teams another state within the same region to study. This time, instruct them to explore all of the categories and record their findings in a new State Study activity.

7. Have teams share their State Study information with the class. Ask students to decide what the states within the same region have in common and have them make generalizations about the region as a whole.

8. Assign students to write a paragraph about the region that focuses on a topic of interest (for example, geographic features or history) and post them on the classroom bulletin board.

(37)

Past and Present

 ## Overview

Investigating the past and comparing it to the present helps students develop a sense of historical perspective and appreciate the effects of technological, philosophical and economic change. In this lesson, students use Kidspiration® to explore and analyze the implications of change.

 ## Standards

- Students understand that daily life is different now from the way it was long ago.

- Students know that technology changes communication, transportation and other aspects of daily life.

- Students read or listen to stories, poems and other media about people and places of other times.

 ## Preparation

1. Gather informational material on daily life in the past.

2. Read stories to students which illustrate daily life in the past. (For example, *The Witch of Blackbird Pond* by Elizabeth George Spears, or any of Laura Ingalls Wilder's *Little House* books.) Spend time discussing "present" versus "past" before reading the stories. Pause at appropriate times during the reading to ask students about elements from the past and how they would be different today.

 ## Lesson

1. Open the Social Studies—Now and Long Ago activity. Remind students of the stories they have read or listened to that were set in the past. Enter ideas volunteered by students into the activity.

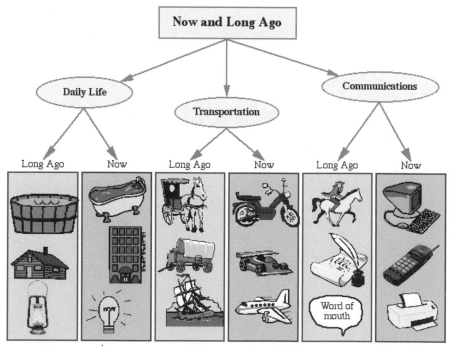

Kidspiration in the Classroom

2. Choose one of the stories you read to the class. Ask students what other categories could be used to examine differences between past and present in the story (for example, the roles of women and children in society, barter versus currency or attitudes toward different cultures).

3. Divide students into teams. Instruct them to open the Social Studies—Now and Long Ago activity and replace the category headings with three new areas for comparison.

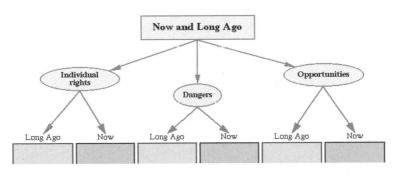

4. Have teams complete the activity using details from the story. Encourage them to look for more ideas in the informational material you gathered, and switch to Writing View to add notes. Circulate to answer questions and check for accuracy.

5. Direct students to open the Reading and Writing—Journal activity and modify it to reflect the place and time of the story. For example, change subtopics to "Chores" or "News."

6. Tell students to imagine that they will be spending one day in the setting of the story they analyzed, and instruct them to complete the Journal activity from that point of view.

7. Have students print their journal entries and create a display in your classroom or school library.

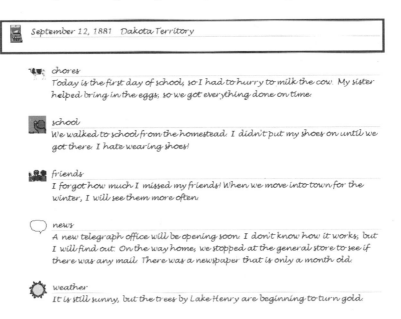

Social Studies | Grades 3-5

The Impact of Exploration

 ## Overview

Exploration and colonization have built and destroyed cultures around the globe. In this lesson, students compare cultures and learn about the effects of a historical encounter.

 ## Standards

• Students know famous explorers and what happened as a result of their travels.

• Students understand the people, events, problems and ideas that were significant in creating the United States of America.

 ## Preparation

Gather informational material on the two cultures to be studied. For example:

• the Native American people of the Chesapeake and Captain John Smith's Europe

• the Celtic people of the British Isles and the Roman Empire

• the native people of Central America and the Spanish culture of Hernando Cortez

 ## Lesson

1. Discuss exploration and explorers with your students. Ask them to speculate about what prompts exploration now compared to long ago.

2. Divide students into teams of two and assign each team to research either the indigenous culture or that of the explorer. Instruct teams to use the informational materials on cultures to study beliefs, economy, government and relationships with neighboring cultures.

3. Have each student pair with a student who studied the other culture. Ask them to open the Social Studies— Culture Comparison activity and record similarities and differences between the cultures.

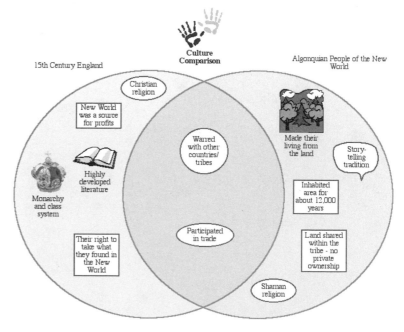

40

4. Guide students to use their Culture Comparison diagram to predict what happened when the cultures made contact. For example, if the commonalities between cultures are warfare or trade, what are the possible outcomes?

5. Share the history of the initial encounters between the cultures. Open the Social Studies—Historical Event activity and use it to demonstrate flow of events, causes and effects and people involved.

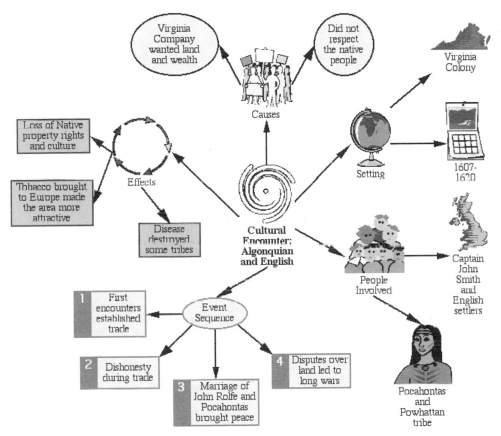

 Extension

Challenge students to write a short monologue from the point of view of one of the participants looking back on the effects of this encounter. Suggest they open a new Social Studies—Historical Event activity and use it to organize their ideas.

Social Studies | Grades 3-5

Historical Heroes

✳ Overview

Every age produces people who are kind, brave and admirable. In this lesson, students investigate a hero from history and use webs and a Venn diagram to analyze and define the concept of heroism.

✳ Standards

• Students know about the lives and contributions of selected men and women from history.

• Students understand that history is the story of events experienced by people in the past.

✳ Preparation

1. Download the A Hero's Life activity and the accompanying Heroes symbol library at www.inspiration.com/kitc or refer to the How To section, pages 102-104, to create your own versions.

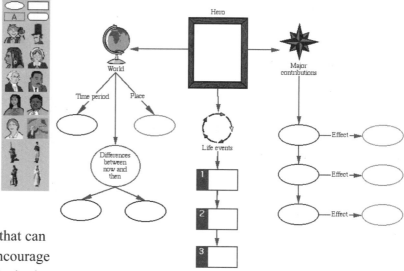

2. Assemble a collection of biographies of respected people from history. Include read-aloud books and books that can be enjoyed independently. Encourage students to look at these books in the week prior to the lesson.

✳ Lesson

1. Open the A Hero's Life activity and demonstrate its use using information from one of the hero biographies you shared with the class.

2. Divide students into teams. Assign them to look through the collection of biographies and choose one hero to analyze.

3. Instruct teams to open the A Hero's Life activity and record their findings.

Kidspiration in the Classroom

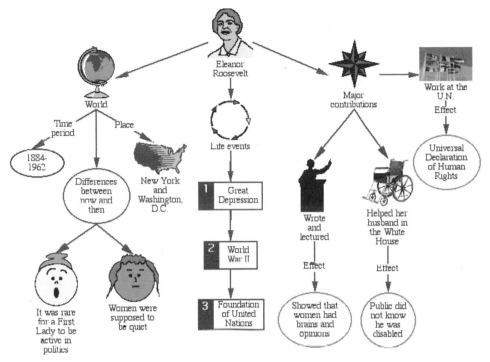

4. Have each student find a partner who analyzed a different hero. Direct them to open the More—Venn Diagram activity and use it to compare the two heroes. Ask them to focus on the heroes' common qualities and how they exemplified them.

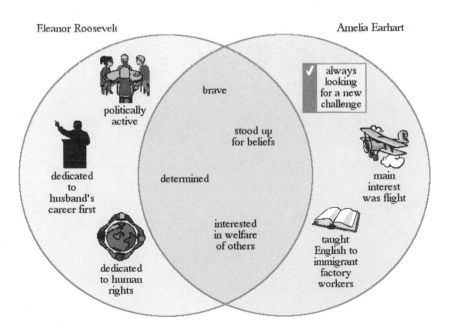

5. Direct pairs to share their diagrams with the class. Discuss heroic qualities and how they translate into action.

 Extension

Have teams create a set of "How to be a Hero" instructions.

Science

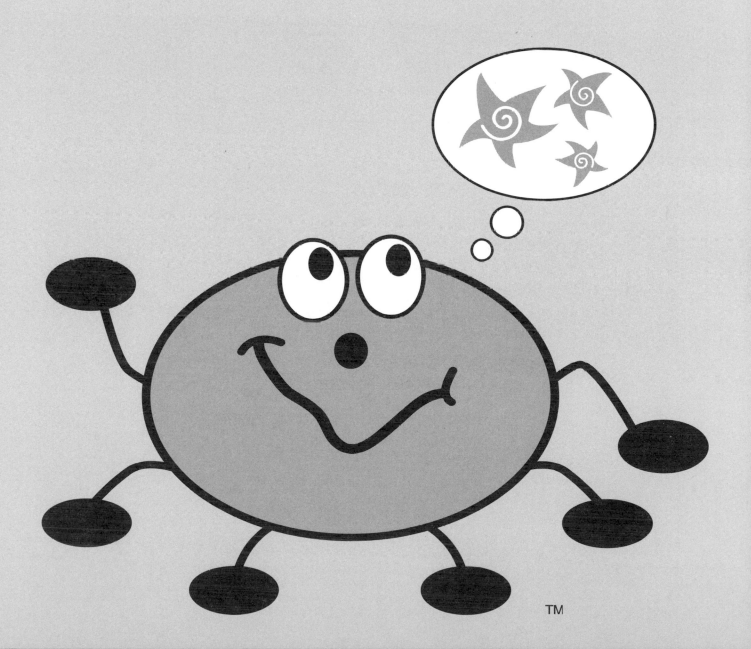

Monitoring the Weather

 ## Overview

Daily weather observation helps students increase their data acquisition skills and develop the use of appropriate scientific instrumentation. In this lesson, students use a graphic organizer to record weather conditions and look for seasonal patterns.

 ## Standards

• Students understand that short-term weather conditions can change daily, but that each season is characterized by general weather patterns.

• Students use simple weather instruments (for example, thermometer, wind vane and rain gauge) to measure and record daily and seasonal changes in the weather.

 ## Preparation

1. Download the Daily Weather Information activity and Monthly Weather Summary activity at www.inspiration.com/kitc or refer to the How To section, page 102, to create your own versions.

2. Construct a rain gauge, a snow gauge and a wind vane. Find instructions for building these instruments on the Internet by entering "simple weather instruments" into a search engine.

3. Place a thermometer outside your classroom window so it is visible to students.

 ## Lesson

1. Tell students they are going to monitor the weather during the school year.

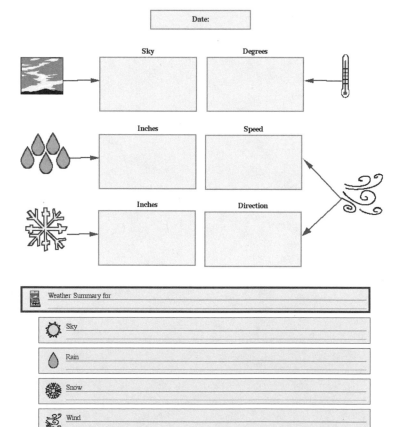

Kidspiration in the Classroom

2. Introduce students to the use of the rain gauge, snow gauge and wind vane.

3. Tell students they will record wind speed as low, moderate and strong. Ask them to decide what they can observe to determine wind speed. For example, in light wind a flag sags around the flag pole, in moderate wind it flutters, and in heavy wind it flies straight out from the pole.

4. Have students form teams of two. Each week, assign a team to record daily weather information.

5. Instruct teams to open the Daily Weather Information activity and record their observations by dragging picture, alphabet and number symbols into the appropriate SuperGrouper® categories.

6. Have teams print the completed activity and post it in the classroom.

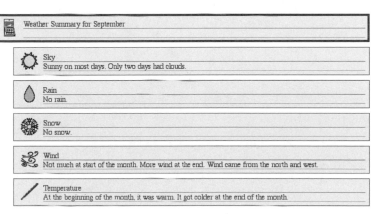

7. At the end of each month, gather the class around the Weather Information diagrams and encourage them to look for patterns in the data. For example, how has the temperature changed over the month? How much rain or snow has fallen over the month? How many days have been sunny or cloudy?

8. Have students open the Monthly Weather Summary activity and record the results of the discussion in the appropriate section. Instruct them to print the summary and collect it in their notebooks.

Weather Summary for September

Sky	Sunny on most days. Only two days had clouds.
Rain	No rain.
Snow	No snow.
Wind	Not much at start of the month. More wind at the end. Wind came from the north and west.
Temperature	At the beginning of the month, it was warm. It got colder at the end of the month.

9. Every three months, ask students to review their summaries and look for seasonal patterns in the weather.

10. At the end of the year, have students compile their monthly summaries into a booklet.

47

Science | Grades K-2

Plant Growth Experiment

✦ Overview

Learning how to design and conduct an experiment is central to science. In this lesson, students use Kidspiration® to plan and carry out a simple experiment on plant growth.

✦ Standards

• Students know the basic growth requirements of animals and plants.

• Students understand that people can often learn about things around them by changing something and observing the results.

✦ Materials Needed

Adjust the amount and type of materials needed depending on your class size and the range of experimental factors.

- Eight-ounce cups
- Seeds (for example, bean, sunflower or pea)
- Sterile sand
- Spring water
- Potting soil
- Cardboard boxes to shield light

✦ Preparation

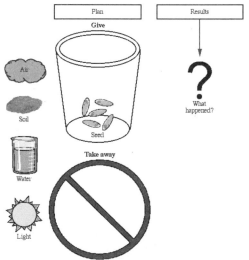

1. Download the Plant Experiment activity at www.inspiration.com/kitc or refer to the How To section, page 102, to create your own version.

2. Gather informational materials on plant growth requirements and review them with students.

✦ Lesson

1. Have the class brainstorm things that plants need to grow.

2. Ask students to decide which of the growth factors they can investigate with the equipment available to them.

3. Inform students they are going to conduct an experiment to determine which factors are the most important for plant growth.

4. Review principles of experimental design with students. In particular, ask them why it is necessary to give some of the plants in the experiment all the growth factors.

48

5. Tell students to form teams and choose a growth factor on which to focus their experiment. Have one team raise plants with all the necessary growth requirements to serve as the control group.

6. Instruct teams to open the Plant Experiment activity and record their experimental design by dragging the growth factor symbols into the appropriate SuperGrouper® categories. Suggest teams switch to Writing View to record more detailed information.

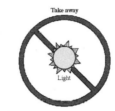

7. Have teams present their designs to the class and encourage students to offer suggestions for improvement.

8. Allow teams to revise their designs as needed.

9. Instruct teams to begin their experiments. Tell them to observe their plants daily. Allow three to four weeks for the experiment, depending on the type of seeds.

10. Have teams open their Plant Experiment diagram and switch to Writing View. Direct them to enter the results of their experiment under the topic labeled, "What happened?"

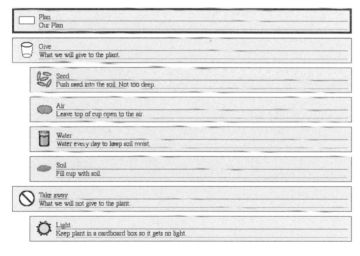

11. Tell students to form groups made up of one member from each team. Ask group members to compare the results of their experiments, and identify which factors seem to be the most important for plant growth. Have students enter the results of their discussion in their Plant Experiment outline under the topic labeled "What is most important for plants?"

	Results
	This is what we found out.

	What happened?
?	The plant was skinny, tall, and white. It looked sick. The plants that had light, soil, air and water were green and healthy.

	What is most important for plants?
	Water and soil, because when they were taken away, the plant did not grow at all.

49

Science | Grades K-2

Motion Study

 ## Overview

Students often observe objects changing motion, but they may not know what causes those changes. In this lesson, students use a Kidspiration® diagram to visualize how changing the magnitude of a force on a toy car affects its motion.

 ## Standard

Students know that the position and motion of an object can be changed by a pull or a push, and the degree of change is related to the magnitude of the pull or the push.

 ## Materials needed

One set per team:

- Two plastic ramps, 15 by 30 centimeters and 15 by 40 centimeters

- Carpet strips to cover the surface of both ramps

- Four two-inch thick blocks

- Toy car

- Tape

- Meter stick

 ## Preparation

Download the Ramp Motion activity at www.inspiration.com/kitc or refer to the How To section, page 102, to create your own version.

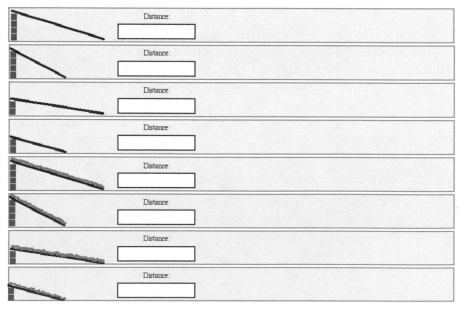

 ## Lesson

1. Demonstrate the experimental procedure by placing one end of the long ramp on a stack of four blocks. Release the car at the top of the ramp and measure how far it travels from the base of the ramp. Repeat the procedure two more times. Demonstrate the same experiment using two blocks to support the long ramp.

50

2. Have students form teams and give each a set of materials.

3. Instruct teams to open the Ramp Motion activity. Tell them to use the toy car to test the following ramp set-ups pictured in the activity:

- Four blocks, long ramp
- Two blocks, long ramp
- Four blocks, short ramp
- Two blocks, short ramp
- The above set-ups with carpet strips taped to the ramp surface

Tell teams to conduct each test three times, measure the distance in centimeters the car travels from the end of the ramp for each trial, and enter the distances into the appropriate symbol in the activity.

4. When teams have tested all the set-ups, ask them to represent the relative position of the car in the diagram by dragging the car symbol into the appropriate SuperGrouper® category for each measurement.

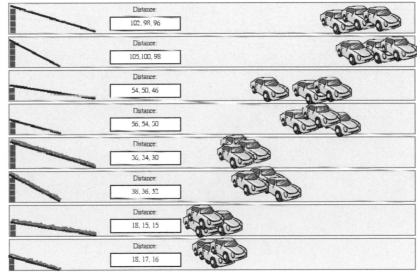

Distance: 102, 98, 96

Distance: 105, 100, 98

Distance: 54, 50, 46

Distance: 56, 54, 50

Distance: 36, 34, 30

Distance: 38, 36, 32

Distance: 18, 15, 15

Distance: 18, 17, 16

5. Instruct teams to print their diagrams and post them in a location where all students can see them.

6. Have the students use the posted diagrams to discuss the following questions:

– Do the distances the car traveled for a single set-up show any variation? Why?

– On which ramp did the car go the farthest? The shortest? Why?

– How could we change a ramp to make the car go farther?

– What would happen to the car if the ramp was flat?

– What force causes the car to move?

51

Science | Grades K-2

Sink or Float

Overview

Describing and categorizing objects according to observable characteristics is an important scientific process. In this lesson, students use a graphic organizer to predict and record observations on the behavior of objects in water.

Standards

• Students know that objects can be described in terms of the materials they are made of and their physical properties.

• Students understand that they can find out about a group of things by studying just a few of them.

Materials Needed

Demonstration materials:

• Fishing weight   • Large tub or bucket

• Birthday candle   • Water

• Wood block

Experimental materials, one set per team:

• Pencil   • Quarter

• Crayon   • Penny

• Orange   • Small tinfoil ball

• Apple   • Cotton ball

• Rock   • Bowl half-filled with water

Preparation

1. Download the Sink or Float activity at www.inspiration.com/kitc or refer to the How To section, page 102, to create your own version.

pencil   crayons   orange   rock   quarter   penny   cotton   apple   tinfoil

✦ Lesson

1. Fill the tub or bucket half full with water, and have students gather around.

2. Invite students to examine the fishing weight, birthday candle and wood block. Ask students to predict which objects will float in water and which will sink.

3. Place the objects in the tub one at a time, and have students observe the results. Ask them if their predictions were correct.

4. Instruct students to form small teams and give each team a set of the experimental materials. Ask them to examine the objects and predict which will sink or float.

5. Tell teams to open the Sink or Float activity and record their predictions by dragging each object symbol into the appropriate SuperGrouper® area.

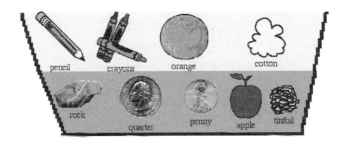

6. Have teams print a copy of their diagram for future reference.

7. Instruct teams to test the experimental objects by placing them in the bowl one at a time. Ask them to record the outcome by adjusting their diagrams as necessary.

8. Ask teams to print copies of their revised diagrams and compare them with their prediction diagrams.

9. Discuss the following questions with students:

   – Did everyone have the same predictions and results?

   – What are the similarities between the items that sank or floated?

   – Did any of the items float lower in the water than others? Why?

   – Why does a boat made out of metal float?

Science | Grades K-2

Advising on Energy

 ## Overview

How is energy produced? What are the trade-offs of various energy production technologies? How should we change energy generation in the future? In this lesson, students research energy production techniques and write a persuasive letter to their legislator.

 ## Standards

- Students know that some energy sources cost less than others and some cause less pollution than others.

- Students understand that the solution to one problem may create other problems.

Preparation

1. Download the Energy Source activity and Energy Policy Advice activity at www.inspiration.com/kitc or refer to the How To section, page 102, to create your own versions.

2. Gather informational material on energy resources and compile a list of related Internet sites such as Energy Quest (http://www.energyquest.ca.gov) and the United States Department of Energy (http://fossil.energy.gov).

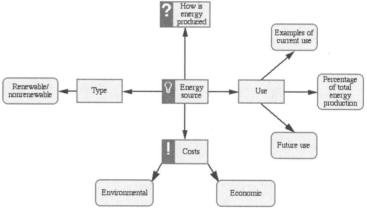

Lesson

1. Have the class brainstorm sources of energy. Open a new Kidspiration® diagram and record their ideas. Contribute any important sources not identified by students.

2. Tell students to form small teams and select an energy source to study.

Kidspiration in the Classroom

3. Instruct teams to research their energy source by consulting the informational material and Internet sites you gathered. Ask them to open the Energy Source activity and enter their findings into the appropriate symbols.

4. Invite teams to present their diagrams to the class. Encourage students to ask questions and offer suggestions.

5. Have teams revise diagrams based on feedback.

Wind turns blades on turbines driving a generator.

Wind farms in states like California and Oregon.

Wind is renewable. It is there as long as the wind blows.

Type

Wind

Use

Less than one percent of current energy production.

Costs

Wind could supply 50 to 60 percent of US electric energy needs.

No chemical pollution. Problems with noise and destruction of scenic values.

Wind power is more expensive than electricity from nonrenewable sources. But it is becoming cheaper as the technology improves.

6. Instruct students to open the Energy Policy Advice activity and use it to write a letter to a local legislator on an issue related to the energy source they researched. For example, a student who researched coal might recommend increased funding for research on converting coal into other fuels, while a student who chose solar energy could advocate for increased use of passive solar construction techniques.

A. Opening
Dear Congressman Jones,

1. My position
We feel that there needs to be more money spent on developing wind power.

a. Supporting statements

(1) Statement
In the future we will need different ways of making electricity.

(a) Reason
Most of our electricity comes from burning oil, coal or natural gas. These are not renewable, and we will run out of them sometime. As we use them up, they will become more expensive.

(2) Statement
We need to reduce air and water pollution formed by burning fossil fuels.

(a) Reason
Coal power plants cause acid rain and smog. Burning fossil fuels makes more carbon dioxide which causes global warming.

7. Have students click the Publish button to finalize their letter in a word processor. Review student work and allow time for further revision.

8. Encourage students to send their letters to their chosen legislator.

55

Birds of Our School

 ## Overview

Central to the study of ecology is the understanding that living things interact with each other and their habitat. In this lesson, students use Kidspiration® to create a web site on the common birds found in the habitats surrounding their school.

 ## Standards

• Students understand that living organisms depend on one another and on their environment for survival.

• Students know that scientific investigations require careful and systematic observation.

 ## Materials needed

• One pair of binoculars for each team

• One copy of a bird identification book for each team

 ## Preparation

1. Download the Bird Observation Record activity and Bird Facts activity at www.Inspiration.com/kitc or refer to the How To section, page 102, to create your own versions.

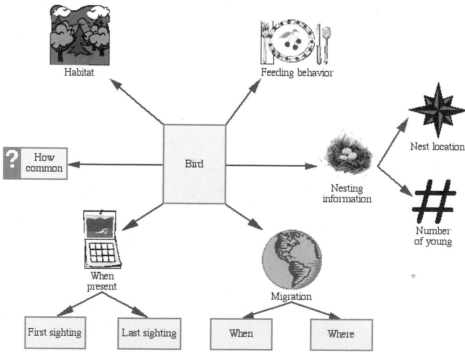

Kidspiration in the Classroom

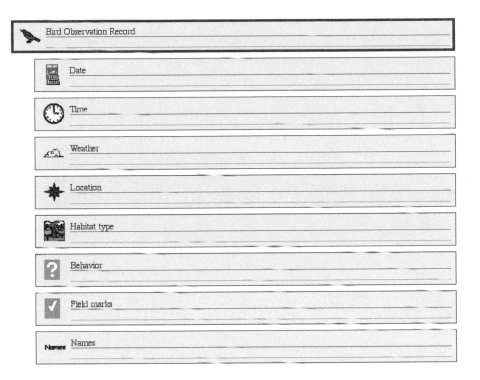

Bird Observation Record

Date

Time

Weather

Location

Habitat type

Behavior

Field marks

Names

2. Gather informational material on local birds, such as species check lists, and compile a list of Internet sites on bird biology and identification such as the USGS Patuxent Bird Identification InfoCenter found at www.usgs.gov.

3. Contact local organizations interested in bird conservation, such as the Audubon Society, and arrange for a volunteer to give a presentation to your students.

Lesson

1. Tell students they will be creating a guide to the birds that frequent the habitats of their school.

2. Have the volunteer give a presentation to your students on the common local birds, bird watching techniques and the use of bird identification books. Ask the presenter to survey the campus with students and help them identify good locations for bird observation.

3. Instruct students to form teams and familiarize themselves with common local birds by consulting the identification manuals and informational material you gathered.

Continued next page

Science | Grades 3-5

4. Assign each team one of the observation locations on campus. Instruct them to open the Bird Observation Record and print a copy for use in the field.

5. Direct teams to observe birds at their assigned location once a week for twenty minutes and record the results of their observations in the Bird Observation Record activity.

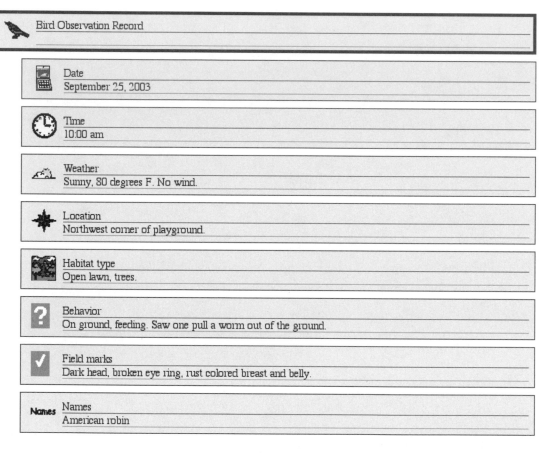

6. Have teams conduct observations for the entire school year, switching locations every two weeks.

7. Towards the end of the school year, instruct teams to use print and Internet materials to further research one of the species they observed. Tell them to open the Bird Facts activity and use it to record their findings. Remind teams to include an image of their bird in the diagram.

8. Have teams share their diagrams with the class. Invite students to offer constructive suggestions for improvement.

9. Tell teams to revise their diagrams based on feedback.

10. Ask teams to use the Export command to export their diagrams as HTML files to serve as the basis for a Birds of Our School web site. Use an HTML authoring program to create a home page to link student diagrams and finalize the web site.

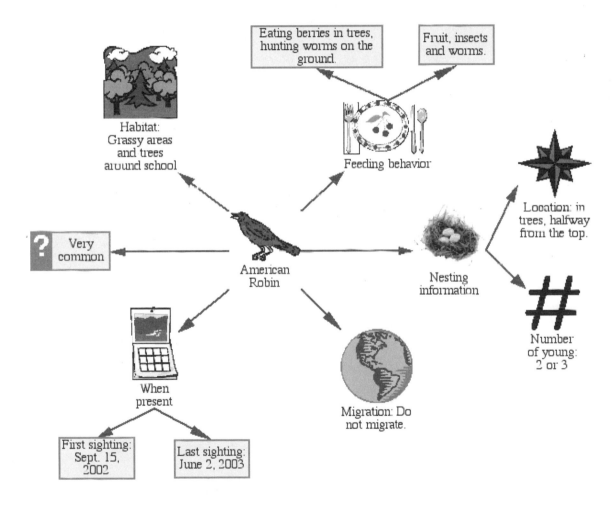

Science | Grades 3-5

Insulation Study

 Overview

Asking questions and devising experiments to find answers is the basis of scientific study. In this lesson, students use Kidspiration® to design an experiment to test the insulating qualities of various materials.

 Standards

• Students know that some materials conduct heat much better than others. Poor conductors can act as insulators.

• Students plan and conduct simple investigations.

 Materials needed

Demonstration materials:

• 250 ml beaker or twelve-ounce cup   • Wood spoon

• Hot water (not boiling)   • Metal spoon

• Plastic spoon

Experimental materials, one set per team:

• 250 ml beaker or eight-ounce plastic cup   • Thermometer

• Aluminum foil   • Stop watch or clock with second hand

• Plastic wrap   • Warm water

• Paper towels

 Preparation

1. Gather informational material on the physics of heat conduction.

2. Review the following principles of experimental design with students:

   – Establishing a control treatment

   – The importance of standardizing treatments. For example, the thickness of insulation and the temperature of the water should be the same for each trial.

   – The need for replication of trials

Kidspiration in the Classroom

Lesson

1. Instruct students to open the Reading and Writing–Vocabulary activity. Have them consult the informational material on the physics of heat conduction to complete the activity for the term "conductor," then repeat the process for the term "insulator."

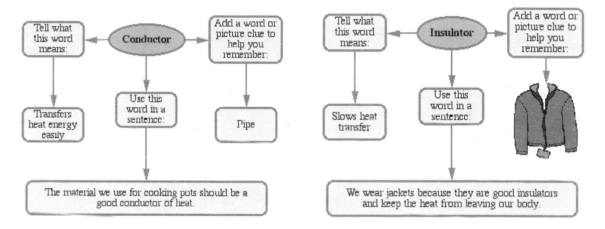

2. In front of the class, pour hot water into the cup and place the plastic, wood, and metal spoons in the cup.

3. Invite students to predict which of the objects in the cup will be the warmest. Ask for a volunteer to test the class's predictions by touching each spoon and describing the sensation. Have students record the results in their notebooks.

4. Divide students into teams, and tell them they are to design an experiment to test which of the experimental materials is the best insulator.

Continued next page

Continued next page

Science | Grades 3-5

5. Instruct teams to open the Science–Experiment activity and describe the steps of their experiment.

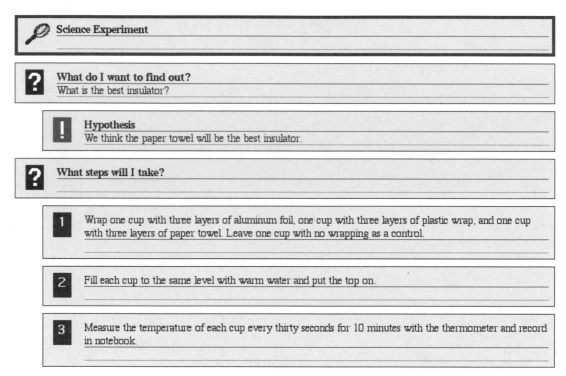

6. Review each team's design before they begin the experiment and offer suggestions as needed.

7. Tell teams to perform the experiment, and have them enter the results of their investigation in their Experiment project.

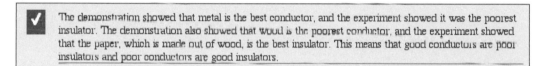

> **? What are the results?**
>
> | 1 | The cup with the aluminum foil and the cup with nothing on it cooled the fastest. |
>
> | 2 | The cup wrapped with plastic cooled off slower than the cup with nothing or aluminum foil, but faster than the cup with paper towel. |
>
> | 3 | The cup wrapped with paper towel cooled off the slowest. |
>
> **? What do they mean?**
>
> | ✓ | The demonstration showed that metal is the best conductor, and the experiment showed it was the poorest insulator. The demonstration also showed that wood is the poorest conductor, and the experiment showed that the paper, which is made out of wood, is the best insulator. This means that good conductors are poor insulators and poor conductors are good insulators. |

8. Ask teams to present their results to the class. Lead a class discussion covering the following points:

– Do teams have differing results? If so, what are possible sources of these differences?

– What is the relationship between a material's ability to conduct heat and its insulating properties?

– How might changing the thickness of the tested materials affect the results?

✳ Extension

Have students design and carry out an experiment to test how the thickness of an insulating material affects the rate of heat loss.

63

Healthy Food Facts

 ## Overview

Understanding the nutritional content of foods encourages healthy eating habits. In this lesson, students create a bulletin board on the benefits of eating fruits and vegetables and present it to a kindergarten class.

 ## Standards

• Students know that food provides energy and materials for growth and repair of body parts.

• Vitamins and minerals, present in small amounts in foods, are essential to keeping bodily functions working well.

 ## Preparation

1. Download the Food Facts activity at www.inspiration.com/kitc or refer to the How To section, page 102, to create your own version.

2. Modify the Reading and Writing–Character Web activity so that it looks like the one shown. Name it Food Benefits and refer to the How To section, page 102, to save it as an activity.

3. Arrange for a local nutrition specialist to talk to your class about the health benefits of eating fruits and vegetables, and the importance of healthy eating habits for young children.

4. Gather informational material on the health benefits of consuming fruits and vegetables, and compile a list of web sites that advocate eating five or more servings of fruits and vegetables a day, such as the National Cancer Institute's 5 A Day for Better Health Program (http://www.5aday.gov).

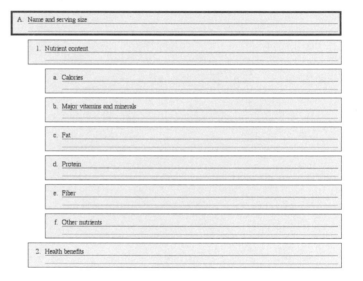

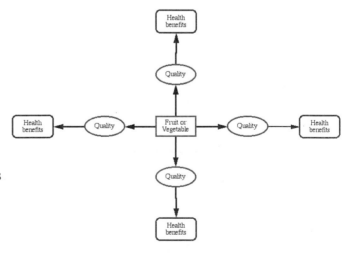

Kidspiration in the Classroom

Lesson

1. Tell students they will be creating a bulletin board on why people should eat fruits and vegetables and presenting it to a kindergarten class.

2. Have the nutrition specialist present to the class the role of fruits and vegetables in a healthy diet, and the importance of developing healthy eating habits early in life.

3. Ask students to form teams and select a fruit or vegetable to research. Instruct teams to use the informational material and web sites you gathered.

4. Direct teams to open the Food Facts activity to record their findings. Remind them to add ideas as needed.

5. Instruct teams to open the Food Benefits activity and use it to create a diagram about the fruit or vegetable they researched which will inform young children on the food's nutritional benefits.

6. Have students form new teams so all fruits and vegetables researched are represented in each team.

7. Tell teams to print their diagrams and compile them into a bulletin board presentation.

8. Arrange for each team to visit a different kindergarten classroom and present their bulletin board to the students.

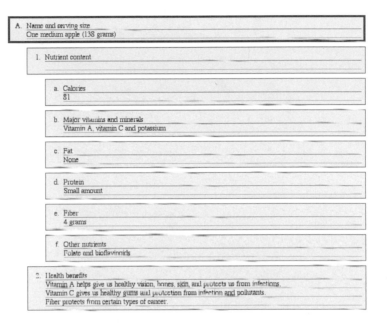

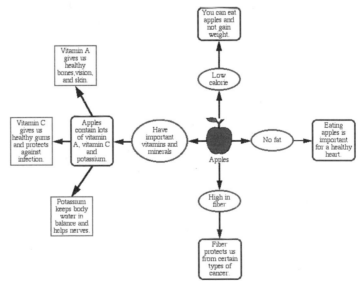

Science | Grades 3-5

Kidspiration in the Classroom

Math

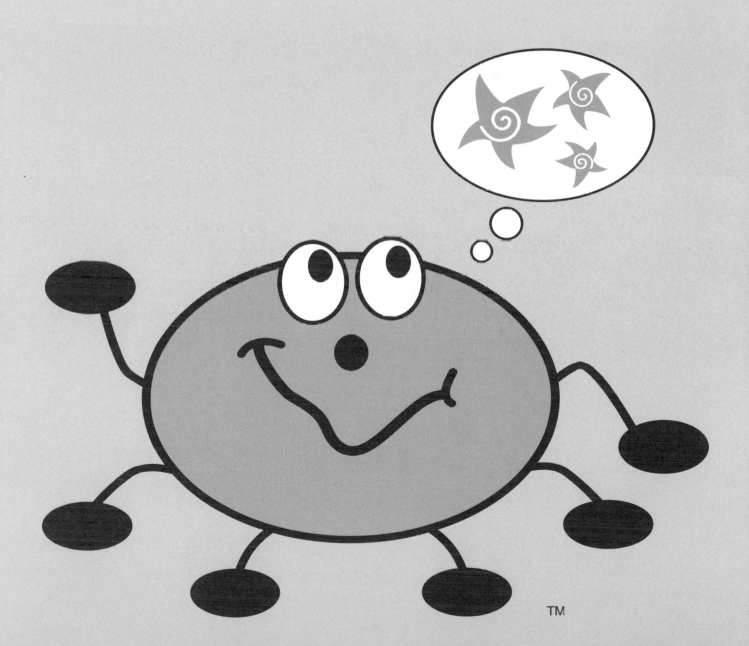

Number and Place

 ## Overview

Understanding place value and the base ten number system is important for further study of mathematics. In this lesson, students use Kidspiration® to represent three place numbers numerically and with base ten units.

 ## Standards

• Students use models to build an understanding of place value and the base ten number system.

• Students connect numerals to the quantities they represent.

 ## Materials needed

A die for each team

 ## Preparation

Download the Number and Place activity and the accompanying Number and Place symbol library at www.inspiration.com/kitc or refer to the How To section, pages 102-104, to create your own versions.

  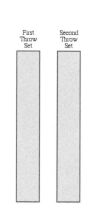 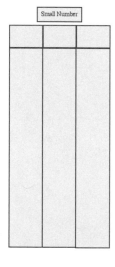

 ## Lesson

1. Have students form teams of two, and instruct them to open the Number and Place activity.

2. Provide a die to each team. Tell teams to create a large and a small three-digit number as follows: throw a die six times and each time drag the resulting number from the symbol library into the First Throw SuperGrouper® set. Tell them to repeat the process for the Second Throw SuperGrouper set.

Kidspiration in the Classroom

3. Instruct teams to create the largest three-digit number possible from the numerals in the First Throw set by dragging them into the appropriate SuperGrouper rectangles at the top of the Big Number table. Remind teams that they will have numbers left over in the throw set.

4. Have teams create the smallest possible three-digit number from the numerals in the Second Throw set by dragging them into the appropriate SuperGrouper rectangles at the top of the Small Number table.

Big Number		
6	5	4

Small Number		
2	3	5

5. Ask teams to drag Hundred symbols into each column under the hundreds place, so that the number of Hundred symbols is equal to the numeral in the hundreds place. Have them follow the same procedure with the Ten symbols under each tens place and the One symbols under each ones place.

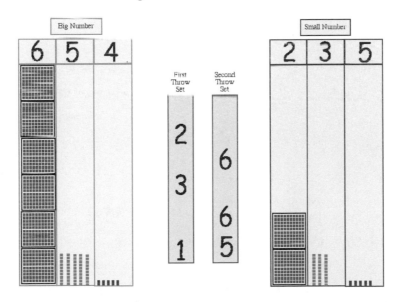

6. Instruct teams to print their diagrams and post them around the room.

7. Encourage students to examine the posted diagrams and identify the biggest and the smallest number produced by the class.

Counting Book

✸ Overview

In this lesson, students develop their counting skills and understanding of number grouping by creating a counting book to represent the value of numbers, 1 through 20.

✸ Standard

Students are able to count with understanding and recognize how many objects are in a given set.

✸ Preparation

Download the Counting Book activities, 1 through 5, and the accompanying Wheels symbol library at www.inspiration.com/kitc or refer to the How To section, pages 102-104, to create your own versions.

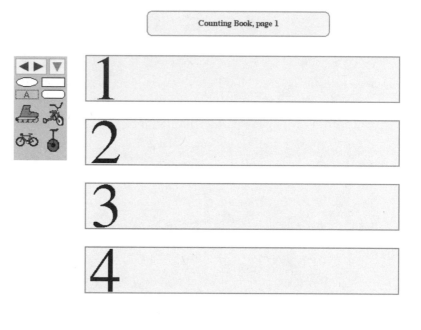

Counting Book, page 1

1

2

3

4

✸ Lesson

1. Open the Counting Book 1 activity and review it with students. Have them identify the number of wheels in each picture on the symbol palette.

2. Model the activity for students by representing the value, four, with wheels: drag the Bicycle and two Unicycle symbols into the SuperGrouper® set containing the numeral, 4. Ask students to suggest other symbol combinations to represent the same value. For each suggestion, delete the current symbols in SuperGrouper set 4, and drag the new symbol combination into the set. Conclude by asking students what is the least number of symbols they can use to show four. To illustrate, drag the skate into set 4.

3. Instruct students to show the value of the numbers, 1 through 20, by opening each of the five Counting Book activities, in turn, and dragging combinations of wheel symbols from the symbol library into the appropriate SuperGrouper sets. The Counting Book 1 activity is for numbers one through four, the Counting Book 2 activity is for numbers five through eight, and so forth.

Kidspiration in the Classroom

4. Inform students that the number of wheels should be the same as the whole number in the SuperGrouper set, and each set should have the smallest number of symbols possible.

5. Ask students to form groups of four and compare their diagrams. Encourage them to find differences in their work and discuss improvements.

6. Provide students time to revise their diagrams if needed.

7. Have students print out each diagram and compile them, in order, into a counting book.

Counting Book, page 1	Counting Book, page 2
1 🛞	5 🛼🛞
2 🚲	6 🛼🚲
3 🛺	7 🛼🛺
4 🛼	8 🛼🛼

8. Question students about the patterns of symbols that appear in their counting books. For example:

How often and when does the bike appear?

– Why does the first SuperGrouper set on each page have a unicycle?

– Will there ever be two numbers in a row that have unicycles?

– Why does the last set on each page contain only skates?

⚜ Extension

Invite students to design another counting book using symbols that show the values, 1 through 5. Encourage them to search the symbol libraries for ideas or use the Symbol Maker to draw their own symbols.

Tell them each page should have five SuperGrouper categories instead of four. Ask students to compare the two activities and look for similarities and differences in the patterns they observe.

71

How Tall is Our Class?

 ## Overview

Asking questions, designing investigations and collecting and analyzing data are broadly applicable skills. In this lesson, students develop these skills by charting the height of all the students in their class.

 ## Standards

• Students develop questions and gather data to answer them.

• Students order and compare objects using such characteristics as length, volume and weight.

• Students select appropriate units and tools for the characteristics being measured.

 ## Materials needed

• One meter stick or yardstick per team

• Assorted measuring devices such as a thermometer, scale and 12-inch ruler

 ## Preparation

1. Download the Class Height activity at www.inspiration.com/kitc or refer to the How To section, page 102, to create your own version. Note: The range of heights represented in this activity is appropriate for an average second grade class. Modify the range of heights as appropriate to your class.

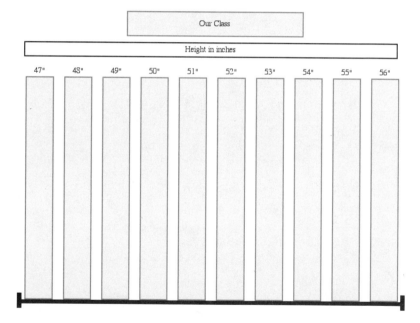

 ## Lesson

1. Have students form teams of four and tell them they are going to answer the question, "How tall are we?"

Kidspiration in the Classroom

2. Show teams the assorted measuring devices, and ask them to discuss which devices they could use to measure the height of students. Have each team share their ideas with the class. Lead a discussion to decide which tool is best suited for measuring height in inches.

3. Have teams measure the height of each team member to the nearest inch. Ask them to record the information on a piece of paper.

4. Instruct teams to open the Class Height activity and record the height and gender for every team member by dragging a symbol of a boy or a girl into the appropriate SuperGrouper category. Suggest they stack symbols from the bottom up.

5. Ask teams to print their diagrams and give a copy to each of the other teams.

6. Tell teams to record the information from other teams in their Class Height diagram so the height of each student in the class is represented in the diagram.

7. Have teams print their final diagrams.

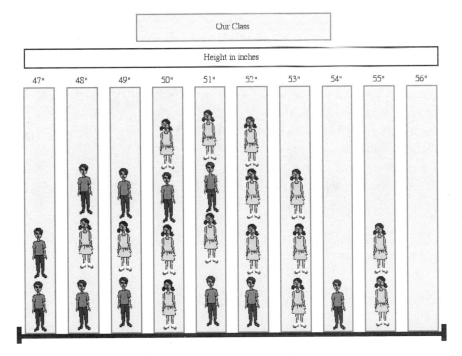

8. Ask teams to refer to their diagrams and discuss the following questions:

– What is the most common height in our class?

– Are there any differences between boys and girls? If so, what are they?

– What do you think the pattern would look like for all second grade students in our school?

Math | Grades K-2

Visualizing Story Problems

Overview

Understanding the relationships between variables in story problems is a crucial step to mathematical understanding. In this lesson, students use Kidspiration® to visualize these relationships and develop computational strategies.

Standards

• Students solve problems that arise in mathematics and in other contexts.

• Students understand various meanings of addition and subtraction of whole numbers and the relationship between the two operations.

• Students develop and use strategies for whole number computations with a focus on addition and subtraction.

Preparation

1. Download the Fish Story Problem activity at www.inspiration.com/kitc or refer to the How To section, page 102, to create your own version.

2. Create several story problems ranging in difficulty from easy to challenging using similar creatures. For example, using tropical fish, you might craft the following problems:

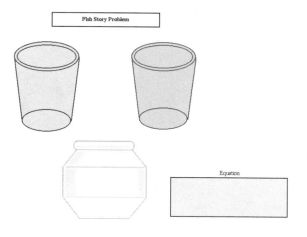

– *Jason purchased three gold fish and three striped fish. He pours each group of fish into his fish bowl. How many fish does he have in the bowl?*

– *Wendy has five gold fish in her fish bowl and puts two into a cup to give to her friend. How many fish are left?*

– *Tameeka has two gold fish in her fish bowl. If each fish has five fins, what is the total number of fins in the bowl?*

Kidspiration in the Classroom

Lesson

1. Open the Fish Story Problem activity and present a sample story problem to students. Ask them how they could use the activity to show the information given in the problem. Model their suggestions as a diagram. Have students suggest how they might visualize possible solutions and modify the diagram accordingly.

Jason purchased three gold fish and three striped fish. He pours each group of fish into his fish bowl. How many fish does he have in the bowl?

Problem diagrammed   **Solution diagrammed**

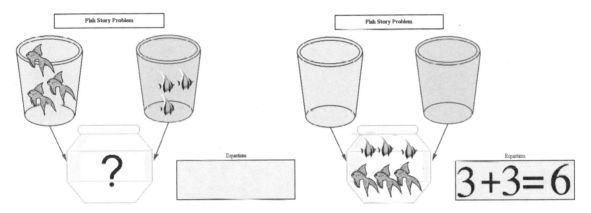

2. Have students form teams of two, and ask them to open the Fish Story Problem activity. Read teams the least difficult story problem, and instruct them to use the activity to picture the information in the story problem by dragging symbols into appropriate SuperGrouper® categories. Have teams print a copy of their diagram.

3. Instruct teams to modify the diagram to represent a visual solution to the problem and an arithmetic expression of the solution by dragging symbols into appropriate SuperGrouper categories. Have them print a copy of their solution.

4. Ask teams to share their printed diagrams with at least two other teams. Different teams will have different ways of representing the problem and its solution. Encourage students to discuss the reasons for their representations.

Continued next page

75

5. Continue this process with the rest of the problems you created. Encourage students to modify the diagram by adding and deleting symbols and SuperGrouper categories as needed.

Wendy has five gold fish in her fish bowl and puts two into a cup to give to her friend. How many fish are left?

Problem diagrammed

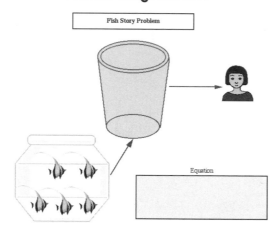

Solution diagrammed

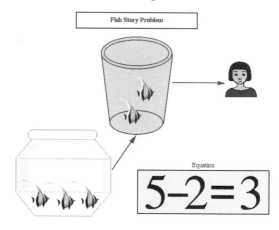

6. Have each team use the Fish Story Problem activity to create a problem to share with the class.

7. Tell teams to drag symbols or numbers into the appropriate SuperGrouper categories to represent the information in their problem.

Jaden can have eight sea creatures in his fish bowl. If he adds four jellyfish, what is the most number of sea horses he can add to the fish bowl?

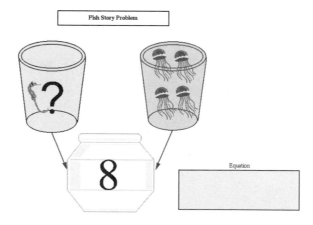

Kidspiration in the Classroom

8. Ask students to print a copy of their story problem for you to review. Allow teams to revise their diagrams as needed.

9. Have teams present their problems to the class. Encourage students to ask questions about the problems.

10. Select several student-created problems and ask teams to diagram solutions using the Fish Story Problem activity.

11. Ask teams to share their solutions with the rest of the class.

 ## Extension

Create story problem sets using other creatures. For example:

– *Emily sees six robins sitting on her front fence. If two of them fly away, how many are left?*

– *Bill's pet guinea pig, Louie, eats three carrots a day. If Bill puts nine carrots in Louie's cage, how many days will they last?*

– *There are five squirrel families living in the park. If each mother squirrel has three babies in the spring, how many baby squirrels are in the park?*

Equivalent Fractions

 ## Overview

Working with equivalent fractions provides insight into such mathematical concepts as ratio and decimal numbers. In this lesson, students create simple webs depicting like fractions.

 ## Standard

Students use models and equivalent forms to judge the size of fractions.

 ## Preparation

Download the Equivalent Fractions activity at www.inspiration.com/kitc or refer to the How To section, page 102, to create your own version.

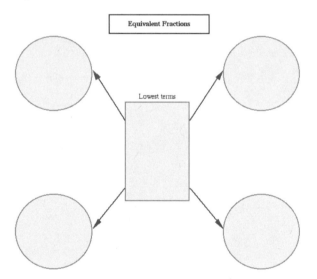

 ## Lesson

1. Instruct students to open the Equivalent Fraction activity, and have them drag the one-half symbol into the lowest terms SuperGrouper® category.

2. Tell students to use the Symbol Maker tool to create visual models of four equivalent fractions, one of which represents the fraction in lowest terms. Instruct students to select an appropriate geometric stamp. Have them use the Line tool to divide the stamp into a number of equal parts suitable for representing the denominator of the fraction they are modeling.

Kidspiration in the Classroom

3. Direct students to represent the numerator of the fraction by filling in the appropriate number of divisions with the Paint Bucket tool.

4. Ask students to place their equivalent fraction symbols in the SuperGrouper circles and label them with the numerical representation of the fraction.

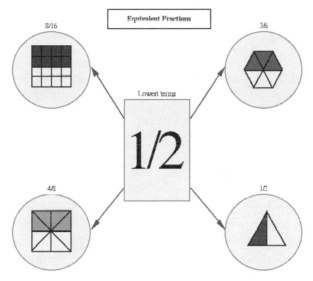

5. Tell students to repeat the process for one-third and one-fourth.

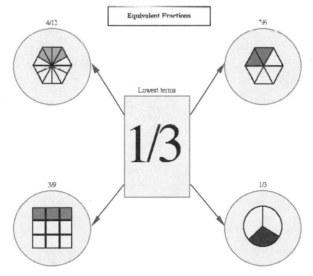

6. Ask students to form small groups and compare their diagrams. Encourage them to offer constructive feedback and suggestions.

7. Have students revise their diagrams as needed.

Progressions

 Overview

Developing an intuitive understanding of exponential functions is helpful for further study of algebra and higher mathematics. In this lesson, students use Kidspiration® to visualize numeric patterns created by simple exponential progressions.

 Standard

Students describe, extend and make generalizations about geometric and numeric patterns.

 Preparation

Download the Clothing Combination activity at www.inspiration.com/kitc or refer to the How To section, page 102, to create your own version.

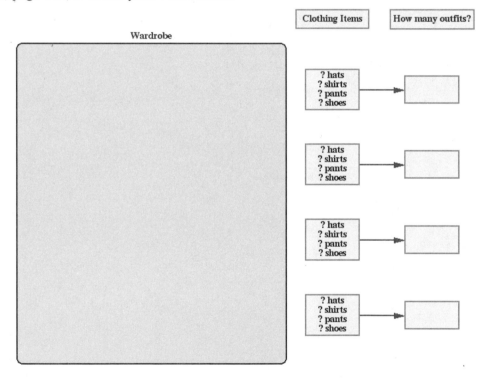

 Lesson

1. Open the Clothing Combination activity and tell students you are going to use it to determine how many complete outfits can be combined from two hats, one shirt, one pair of pants and one pair of shoes. Enter the number for each item of clothing into the first Clothing Items symbol.

Kidspiration in the Classroom

2. Drag symbols representing articles of each type of clothing into the Wardrobe SuperGrouper® category and use the Link tool to show the possible combinations of clothing items. For instance, in the diagram below, the links show that the stocking cap and the baseball cap can each be worn with the rest of the outfit for a total of two outfits. Enter the number of outfits into the appropriate symbol.

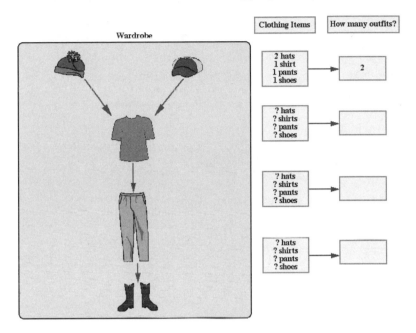

3. Add another shirt to the SuperGrouper category and repeat the process. Now that there are more links, discuss with students strategies for tracing the connecting paths of links to determine the number of possible outfits. Again, enter the number into the appropriate symbol.

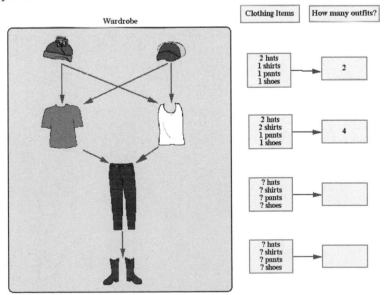

Continued next page

Math | Grades 3-5

4. Have students form teams of two and open the Clothing Combination activity.

5. Instruct teams to reproduce the progression you started and continue it by dragging another pair of pants into the SuperGrouper category and adding links. Have them determine the number of outfit combinations, then add another pair of shoes and repeat the process.

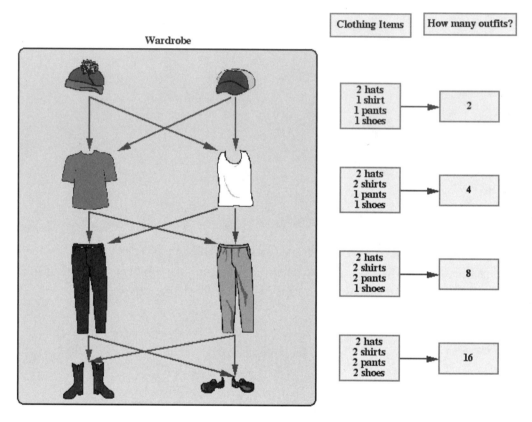

Wardrobe

Clothing Items	How many outfits?
2 hats 1 shirt 1 pants 1 shoes	2
2 hats 2 shirts 1 pants 1 shoes	4
2 hats 2 shirts 2 pants 1 shoes	8
2 hats 2 shirts 2 pants 2 shoes	16

6. Ask teams to print their diagrams.

7. Tell teams to open a new Clothing Combination activity and complete it for the following progression:

– Three hats, one shirt, one pair of pants, one pair of shoes

– Three hats, three shirts, one pair of pants, one pair of shoes

– Three hats, three shirts, three pairs of pants, one pair of shoes

– Three of each item of clothing. Note: at this point, students will likely have difficulty counting all the possible outfits. Encourage students to examine the pattern of increase and predict how many outfit combinations can be produced.

82

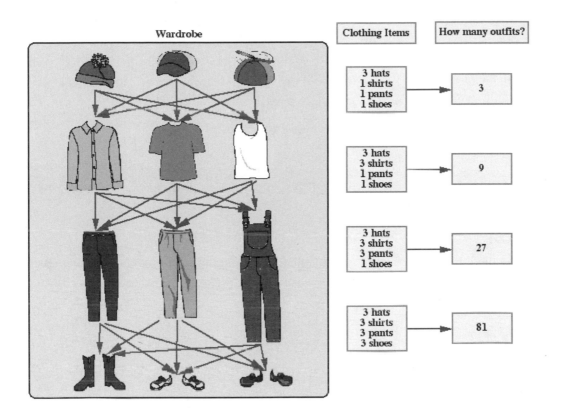

Wardrobe

Clothing Items	How many outfits?
3 hats 1 shirts 1 pants 1 shoes	3
3 hats 3 shirts 1 pants 1 shoes	9
3 hats 3 shirts 3 pants 1 shoes	27
3 hats 3 shirts 3 pants 3 shoes	81

8. Have teams print their new diagrams.

9. Ask each team to meet with at least three other teams and share their diagrams. Have the larger groups discuss the following questions:

– Which clothing diagram results in the most rapid increase in possible combinations? The slowest? Why?

– Without creating a diagram, how might they determine the number of possible outfits for four hats, four shirts, four pairs of pants, and four pairs of shoes?

Extension

Ask students to discuss how they might represent the patterns they observe using an equation. Guide the discussion toward an exponential representation.

Functions

 Overview

The understanding of mathematical functions forms a crucial foundation for the study of algebra and higher mathematics. In this lesson, students derive functions from numerical patterns and demonstrate their understanding of the function concept.

 Standards

- Students understand patterns, relations and functions.

- Students use and interpret variables, mathematical symbols and properties to write expressions and sentences.

 Preparation

1. Download the Function Generator activity, Function Definition activity and the accompanying Number and Place symbol library at www.inspiration.com/kitc or refer to the How To section, pages 102-104, to create your own versions.

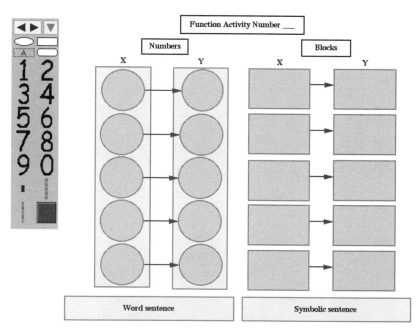

2. Use the Function Generator activity to create several different activities for students by entering x and y values for simple addition, subtraction, multiplication and division functions into the appropriate symbols. Here is a sample of an activity created for the function, x + 6 = y:

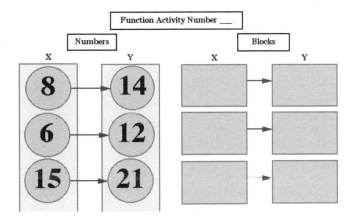

Function Activity Number ___

Numbers

Blocks

Refer to the How To section, page 102, to save each file as an activity. Name and organize the Function Generator activities so students will open the simplest function first and progress to more difficult functions.

 Lesson

1. Open a Function Generator activity you created and model its use for students. Drag base ten pieces into the appropriate SuperGrouper® categories and ask students to look for a pattern.

2. With the class, develop both a word and symbolic sentence to describe the pattern, and enter those sentences into the appropriate symbols.

3. Have students open the first Function Generator activity and complete it.

4. Ask students to form small groups and share their diagrams with each other. Encourage students to discuss their reasoning and compare their results. Have students revise their diagrams as necessary.

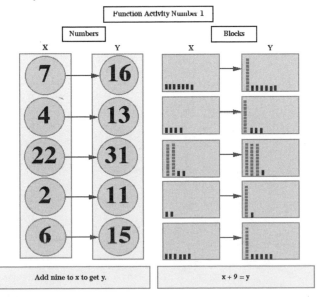

Function Activity Number 1

Numbers

Blocks

Add nine to x to get y. $x + 9 = y$

Math | Grades 3-5

Grouping Numbers

Overview

Modeling numbers in a variety of ways is a useful activity for study of advanced mathematics. In this lesson, students explore the commutative and distributive properties by representing numbers with rectangular arrays.

Standard

Students can identify the commutative and distributive properties and use them to compute with whole numbers.

Preparation

Download the Array Grouping activity and the accompanying Number Pieces symbol libraries at www.inspiration.com/kitc or refer to the How To section, pages 102–104, to create your own versions.

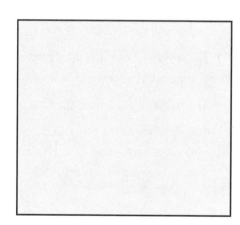

Lesson

1. Open the Array Grouping activity and drag number piece symbols into each SuperGrouper® shape to create a three by five rectangular array and a five by three rectangular array as pictured below. Label each SuperGrouper shape with the appropriate arithmetic expression. Discuss with students whether the arrays have the same number of squares. Use the Link tool to show the relationship between the two arrays.

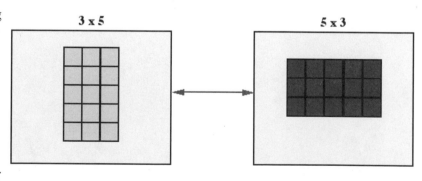

3 x 5   5 x 3

Kidspiration in the Classroom

2. Repeat the process for at least two other arrays, such as five by ten and eight by six.

3. Explain to students that the ability to change the order of numbers in an expression without changing the result is known as the commutative property. Lead a class discussion on the use of the property in addition and multiplication.

4. Open a new Array Grouping activity and construct an eight by six array in the first SuperGrouper shape as pictured below. Ask students to suggest a way of "splitting" the array into two smaller arrays. Represent their ideas by dragging symbols into the second shape. Label each shape with an arithmetic expression that symbolically describes its contents. Use the Link tool to connect the shapes.

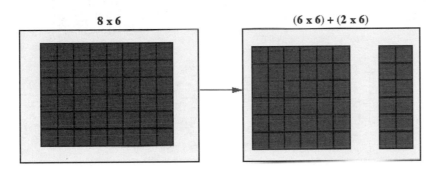

5. Inform students that this is one model of the distributive property, and lead a class discussion on the use of the property in addition and multiplication.

6. Have students form teams of two and open the Array Grouping activity.

Continued next page

Math | Grades 3-5

7. Instruct teams to explore ways of regrouping arrays such as five by six, seven by eight, and nine by four. Ask them to create combinations of two smaller arrays by splitting the original array either horizontally or vertically. Have them label each SuperGrouper shape with an arithmetic expression that describes the contents of the shape. Encourage them to add, move or resize SuperGrouper shapes as needed, and use more than one Array Grouping activity to represent other combinations.

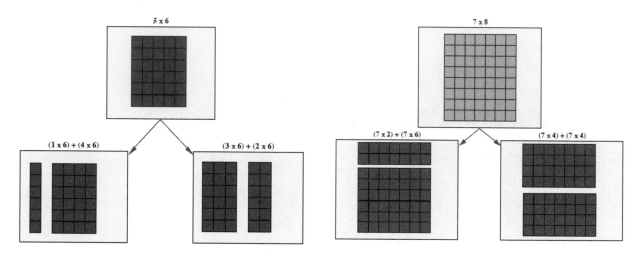

8. Ask each team to print diagrams which present the most variety of groupings derived from a single array. Have teams present their diagrams to the class and discuss their work.

9. During the presentations, point out how the commutative and distributive properties can be used to create different representations of numbers. Close by soliciting ideas on how students might use the distributive property to compute a more difficult multiplication problem such as 12×50.

Teaching Resources

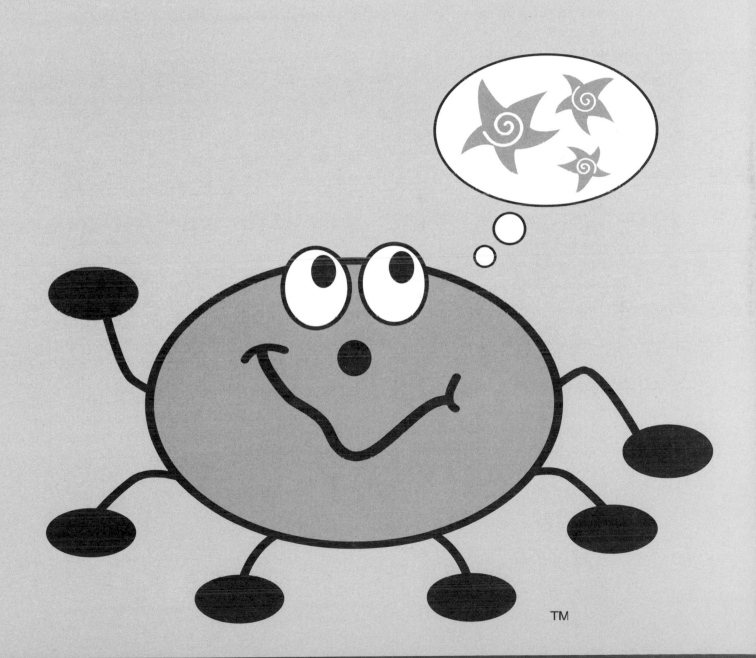

Concept Mapping

 ## Overview

Concept maps encourage understanding by helping students organize and enhance their knowledge on any topic. They help students learn information by integrating each new idea into their existing body of knowledge.

Concept maps are ideal for measuring the growth of student learning. As students create concept maps, they restate ideas using their own words. Misdirected links or wrong connections alert educators to what students do not understand, providing an accurate, objective way to evaluate areas in which students do not yet grasp concepts fully.

 ## Preparation

Discuss with students the purpose and attributes of a concept map. Show several examples of varying complexity.

 ## Lesson

1. Identify a single concept upon which to base a concept map. For example, in the study of geography, students might start with the concept, "desert."

2. Open Kidspiration® and enter the concept into the Main Idea symbol.

3. Ask students to volunteer associated ideas, concepts or topics and enter them into the diagram.

sand

hot

empty

cactus

coyotes

desert

camels

dry

snakes

lizards

4. Show students how
to use the Link tool
to link related
symbols. In each
link's associated
text box, enter
words that explain
the relationship
between the ideas.
To aid student
thinking, remind
them that in a
concept map it is
possible to read
symbols and their
connecting link text
as sentences.
Encourage students
to add concepts
as needed.

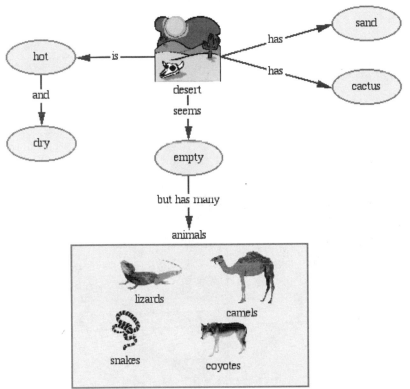

✴ Concept Map activity

The Science—Animal Concept Map activity or More—Concept Map activity offer students
additional ways to develop a concept map.

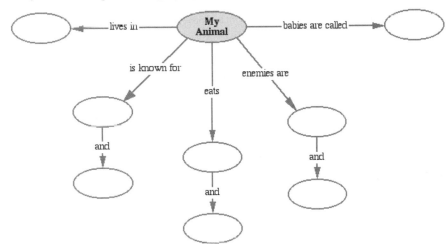

Use the Activity Wizard to modify this concept map to suit other areas of the curriculum.

Teaching Resources

Designing Rubrics

Rubrics can be challenging to design, but once in place, they save time and clarify expectations. Here is a simple process for creating your own rubrics with Kidspiration®:

1. Download the Rubric activity at www.inspiration.com/kitc or refer to the How To section, page 102, to create your own version.

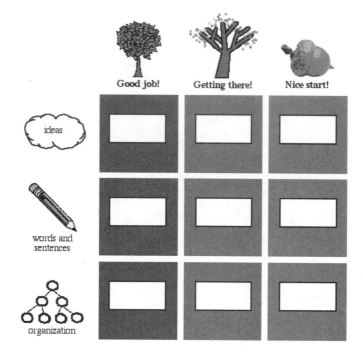

2. Make a preliminary decision on the elements to be assessed and modify the Rubric activity as necessary. Look at student work samples to see if you have omitted any important areas for assessment.

3. Write brief descriptions of each performance level and enter them into the appropriate areas.

Kidspiration in the Classroom

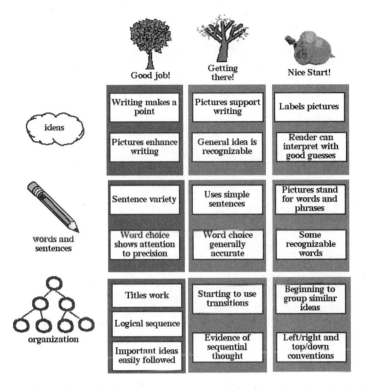

4. If appropriate, share the rubric with your students before they begin their assigned project.

5. Following the assignment, indicate performance levels on the rubric.

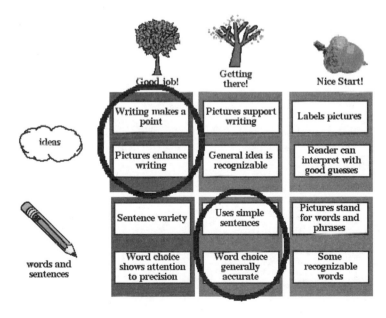

6. To address different assignments, experiment with rubric layouts and ways of representing information.

Continued next page

Teaching Resources

Designing Rubrics
continued

✪ More examples:

Team project

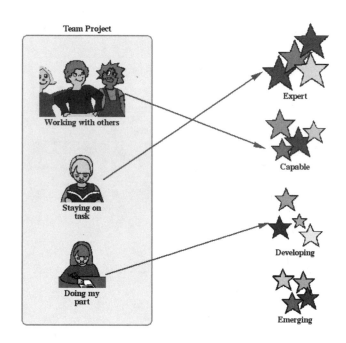

Team Project

Working with others

Staying on task

Doing my part

Expert

Capable

Developing

Emerging

Science experiment

Science Experiment

Level	Hypothesis	Design	Results	Writing
Excellent	Experimental question is specific, hypothesis relates directly to it	All parts present. Control, if needed, present	Results clearly displayed in a table and graph	Writing is clear and concise. Grammar and spelling correct
Good job	Question is specific, hypothesis is not directly related to it	Most parts present, including control	Results displayed in table and graph with some small errors	Writing is clear, a few minor errors in grammar and spelling
Nice start	Question is not specific, hypothesis is either not related or absent	Serious errors in design, control missing	Errors in results table and graph make it hard to determine the outcome	Writing is confusing and hard to follow. Major errors in grammar and spelling
Not yet	Question is so broad that it cannot be answered, or absent	Unable to follow how experiment will be done	Table and graph either absent or cannot be understood	Writing is so confusing and full of errors that it cannot be understood

94

Math problem

Math problem

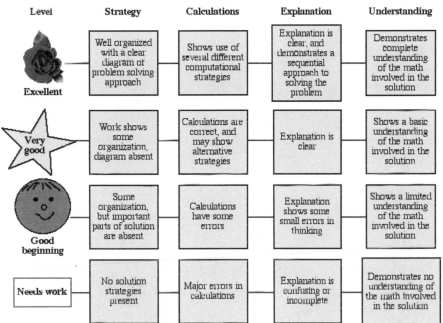

Level	Strategy	Calculations	Explanation	Understanding
Excellent	Well organized with a clear diagram of problem solving approach	Shows use of several different computational strategies	Explanation is clear, and demonstrates a sequential approach to solving the problem	Demonstrates complete understanding of the math involved in the solution
Very good	Work shows some organization, diagram absent	Calculations are correct, and may show alternative strategies	Explanation is clear	Shows a basic understanding of the math involved in the solution
Good beginning	Some organization, but important parts of solution are absent	Calculations have some errors	Explanation shows some small errors in thinking	Shows a limited understanding of the math involved in the solution
Needs work	No solution strategies present	Major errors in calculations	Explanation is confusing or incomplete	Demonstrates no understanding of the math involved in the solution

Teaching Resources

Symbol Maker Ideas

Using the Symbol Maker tool, students can express their unlimited visual vocabulary by drawing and painting their own symbols. Research shows that drawing increases activity in the brain, helping young students generate and connect ideas. As with writing, students make decisions and solve problems when they draw. Drawings in Kidspiration® become an important element of student graphic organizers, allowing young learners to refine and personalize meaning.

Uses for the Symbol Maker tool are as varied as the students in your classes. Here are some ideas to get you started:

Create a class portrait gallery:

Depict story elements for writing:

Personalize information about daily life:

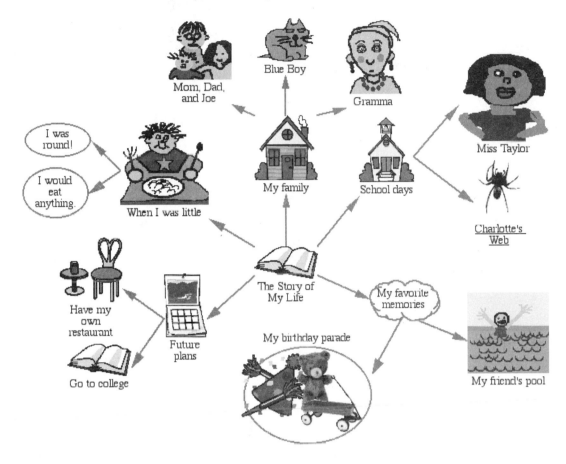

Develop visual memory cues:

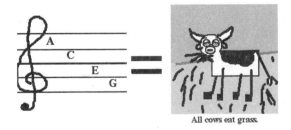

Continued next page

97

Teaching Resources

Symbol Maker Ideas
continued

Create symbols to extend a custom library:

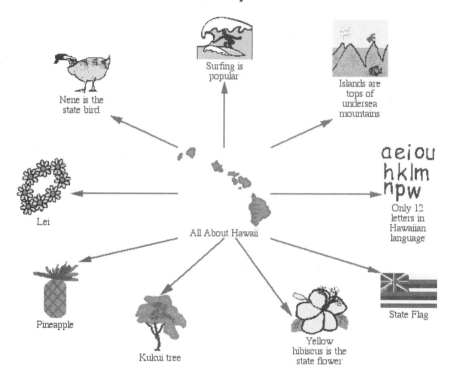

Record daily observations for science:

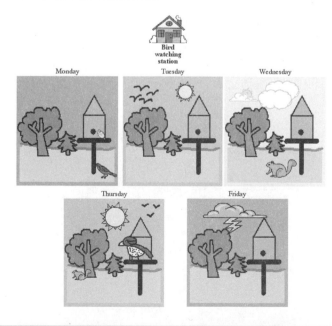

Kidspiration in the Classroom

Illustrate experimental procedures:

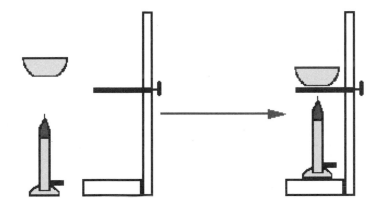

Design manipulatives for mathematical investigations:

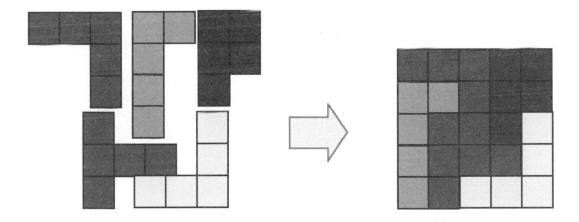

99

Kidspiration in the Classroom

How To

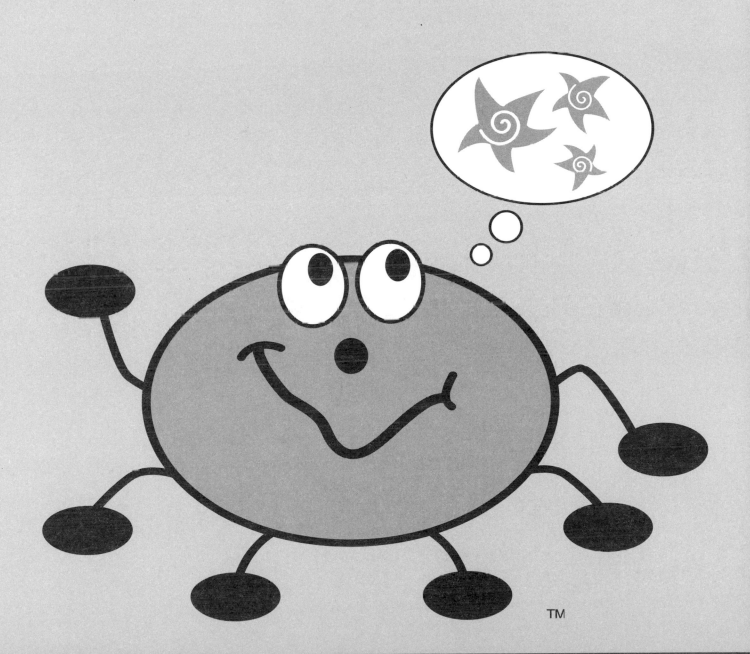

How to Create Activities

You can create a project in Picture View or Writing View, and then save it as an activity so it will be available in the Activities menu in the Kidspiration® Starter. You can also save an activity in another location, such as on a server, so it can be shared by a classroom of students.

 To create an activity:

1. Create the project in Picture View or Writing View. (See Tips below for creating activities.)

2. Enable the Teacher menu.

3. On the Teacher menu, click Save With Activity Wizard.

4. Select All Libraries or Selected Libraries:

   – Select All Libraries to make all libraries available, or

   – Select Selected Libraries to make selected libraries available.

     • To remove a library from the list of available libraries.

     • To remove all libraries from the list of available libraries, click Remove ALL.

     • To make a library available, click it in the list, and then click Select.

5. Select the default settings you want for the activity.

6. In the Activity Name box, type a name for the activity.

7. In the Description of Activity box, type a description for the activity. The description appears when you select from the list of activities.

8. Select the folder where you want to save the activity:

   – To save the activity on the same computer where the Kidspiration program is installed, select Kidspiration Activities Folder. Click the category you want the activity to appear under, for example "Science," and then click Save Activity.

   – To save the activity to a location other than the computer where the Kidspiration program is installed, select Another Location (for example, a server). Click Save Activity. Navigate to the folder where you want to save the activity.

Kidspiration in the Classroom

Tips

Numbered Steps: Many of the Kidspiration activities include step-by-step instructions. To create numbered steps in your own activities, use the numbered symbols under Numbers and Letters on the Symbol palette.

Lock Items: Freeze the position of items, for example SuperGrouper® shapes in an activity, using the Locked Item command on the Teacher menu. Locking items prevents students from accidentally moving, replacing or deleting specific symbols or SuperGrouper shapes.

Custom Symbol Libraries: If you want specific symbols to be available for an activity, you can create a custom symbol library that contains the symbols you want, and then select the custom library as the Default Library for the activity. Note: The custom symbol library must be copied to each computer.

Publish Options: In the Kidspiration Activity Wizard, select the options that control how the project looks when you transfer it to a word processor using the Publish tool.

How to Create New Symbol Libraries

You can create new symbol libraries for symbols you import, create or copy from other libraries. For example, you might want to create a new symbol library for the symbols you use frequently or for an activity that you create. You can place a new symbol library under any category on the Symbol palette. If you do not choose a category, the symbol library is automatically stored in the Custom category.

 To create a new symbol library:

1. Enable the Teacher menu.

2. On the Teacher menu, click New Symbol Library.

3. In the Category list, select the category that you want the new library to appear under on the Symbol palette.

4. In the Library box, type a name for the new library.

5. On the Teacher menu, click Edit Symbol Libraries.

6. Use the tools in this dialog to add new symbols to your library.

Kidspiration in the Classroom

How to Use the Publish Tool

You can use the Publish tool to transfer a project in Writing View to Microsoft® Word or AppleWorks®. You can control how projects are published using the publish options (click Publish Options on the Teacher menu). You can also set publish options when you choose default settings for a project and when you save a project as an activity.

In the word processing document, ideas and notes text appear on separate lines with no indentation. Ideas are the text size of the Writing View default font with bold formatting. Notes are the text size of the Writing View default font. A blank line appears between each note card.

 ## To transfer a project to a word processor:

On the Formatting toolbar, click the Publish button.

The Kidspiration project is transferred to the word processing document. The preferred word processor starts and opens the document.

The word processing document is saved in one of the following locations:

– If you save the Kidspiration project before you publish it, the word processing document is saved in the same folder as the Kidspiration project.

– If you do not save the Kidspiration project before you publish it, the word processing document is saved in the user Documents folder (Mac OS X), the root Documents folder (Mac OS 9) or My Documents folder (Windows).

How to Use the SuperGrouper® Tool

One of the first skills that children are taught in school is sorting and categorizing. Whether separating blocks with numbers from those with letters, or sorting items by shape and color, learning how to recognize basic attributes of simple ideas fosters the ability to analyze those that are more complex.

When students drag a symbol to a SuperGrouper® category, it automatically becomes a subset both visually and verbally. The symbols move with the SuperGrouper® category that contains them. In Writing View, the ideas are listed under the name of the SuperGrouper category.

Adding a SuperGrouper shape to a diagram

1. On the Picture toolbar, click the SuperGrouper button.

2. Click the SuperGrouper shape you want to add to the diagram.

Tip: Any symbols that are selected when you add a SuperGrouper category are automatically added to the SuperGrouper category.

Adding a Venn diagram SuperGrouper shape

The Venn diagram SuperGrouper shape is a diagram composed of two circles that overlap in the middle. It can be used in lessons where students identify and categorize differences and similarities between objects and ideas.

1. On the Picture toolbar, click the SuperGrouper button.

2. On the SuperGrouper menu, click Venn.

The Venn diagram SuperGrouper category appears on your diagram. You can change the "Group A" and "Group B" titles and begin adding symbols to each area of the diagram.

Creating a SuperGrouper shape

Any symbol can be transformed into a SuperGrouper shape.

1. Select the symbol.

2. On the Picture toolbar, click the SuperGrouper button.

3. On the SuperGrouper menu, click Create SuperGrouper.

 ## Adding symbols to a SuperGrouper category

You can add symbols to a SuperGrouper category using any of the following methods:

– Drag a symbol to the SuperGrouper category.

– Select the SuperGrouper category, and then click the Add Symbol button.

– Select the symbols that you want to add to the SuperGrouper category, and then add the SuperGrouper category to your diagram.

Suggested Reading

Anders, G. & Beech, L.W. (1990). *Reading: Mapping for meaning*. Kent, CT: Sniffen Court Books.

Bromley, K.D. (1995). *Webbing with literature: Creating story maps with children's books*. Needham Heights, MA: Allyn & Bacon.

Bromley, K.D., Irwin-DeVitis, L., et al. (1995). *Graphic organizers: Visual strategies for active learning*. New York, NY: Scholastic, Inc.

Douglas, K., et al. (2003). *Teaching K-6 mathematics*. Mahwah, NJ: Lawrence Erlbaum Associates.

Graves, D. (1983). *Writing: Teachers and children at work*. Portsmouth, NH: Heinemann.

Green, P.A. (Ed.). (1995). *Graphic organizer collection*. Palatine, IL: Novel Units.

Hansen, J. (2001). *When writers read*. Portsmouth, NH: Heinemann.

Harste, J., et al. (1984). *Language stories and literacy lessons*. Portsmouth, NH: Heinemann.

Jonassen, D.H. (1996). *Computers in the classroom: Mindtools for critical thinking*. Englewood Cliffs, NJ: Merrill.

Llewellyn, D. (2002). *Inquire within: Implementing inquiry-based science standards*. Thousand Oaks, CA: Corwin Press, Inc.

Marzano, R.J., Pickering, D.J. & Pollock, J.E. (2001). *Classroom instruction that works: Research-based strategies for increasing student achievement*. Alexandria, VA: Association for Supervision and Curriculum Development.

Novak, J.D. & Gowin, D.B. (1984). *Learning how to learn*. New York, NY: Cambridge University Press.

Rothlein, L. and Meinbach, A. (1991). *The literature connection*. Glenview, IL: Scott Foresman and Company.

Routman, R. (1988). *Transitions: From literature to literacy*. Portsmouth, NH: Heinemann.

Thomas, James L. (1992). *Play, learn, and grow: An annotated guide to the best books and materials for very young children*. New Providence, NJ: R.R. Bowker.

Thornburg, D.D. (1998). *Brainstorms and lightning bolts: Thinking skills for the 21st century*. San Carlos, CA: Starsong Publications.

About the Authors

Mary Chase, Ph.D.

Mary Chase, Ph.D., earned her doctorate in Literacy and Schooling from the University of New Hampshire. After a career in public school teaching, she taught writing and literature at the University of Puget Sound, and courses in teacher education at Pacific Lutheran University. As a curriculum designer at Inspiration Software, Inc., Dr. Chase's background in theory and practice informs the development of new products and other educational materials. Her articles have appeared in *Language Arts* and the *Quarterly of the National Writing Project*.

Bob Madar

Bob Madar is a curriculum designer for Inspiration Software, Inc. with 14 years experience teaching science at the high school level. He earned his M.S. in Entomology at Oregon State University. In 1997, he received a McAuliffe award for excellence in science teaching, and in 1999, his field studies course was featured in "Learning that Works" produced by WGBH. Mr. Madar has also provided training in inquiry-based science instruction, project-based learning and small learning community development to schools and school districts throughout the United States.

Lesson Plan Books

Successfully integrate visual learning into your classroom

Discover a wealth of ideas to engage learners and improve performance with activities that encourage students to learn, think and create. Educators new to using Kidspiration® and Inspiration® get started integrating visual learning more quickly and effectively, veteran users are inspired with new ideas, and trainers are able to customize workshops with examples specific to any audience.

Convenient, ready-to-use templates for a variety of lessons are available online.

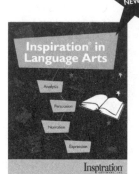

Inspiration in Language Arts
Standards-aligned lesson plans
Improve language arts outcomes with these 30+ standards-based lesson plans covering analysis, persuasion, narration and expression for grades 6-12. Many lessons such as "Literary Comparison" can be used again with different content.

Inspiration in Science:
Standards-aligned lesson plans
30+ lesson plans cover life, physical and earth sciences. 6th to 12th grade students build concept maps, develop experimental designs and lab reports and implement assessment strategies. Lessons include "States of Matter" and "DNA Fingerprinting."

Achieving Standards with Inspiration 7
Curriculum-aligned lessons for inspired learning
Teachers get started using Inspiration effectively with this set of 35 lesson plans for middle and high schoolers in language arts, social studies and science. Lessons include "Visualizing Meaning in Poetry," "Cause and Effect in History" and "Lunar Cycle."

Kidspiration in the Classroom

Interactive Training CDs

Step-by-step instruction at your own pace

Our interactive, narrated training CDs introduce you to the world of Kidspiration, Inspiration and visual learning. This popular multimedia format lets you learn when your schedule permits—at your own pace. Follow along through the complete step-by-step training or jump to a particular topic or practical classroom example.

Use the Exploring CDs for individual training, to supplement your in-service training sessions or for ready reference about specific Kidspiration 2 or Inspiration 7 features and functions.

What's included?
- Visual learning methodologies
- Narrated step-by-step tutorial
- Curriculum-specific examples

Want to share these great lesson plans?

Special Volume Pricing

Now it is easy and cost-effective to assure you are getting the most out of Kidspiration® , Inspiration® and visual learning within your school or across your district. Our standards-based lesson plans help teachers take advantage of the power of visual learning and improve achievement across language arts, science, math and social studies.

Electronic Format

All of our lesson plan books are now available in an easy-to-share electronic format. When you purchase a volume license, you receive a bound copy of the lesson plan book and a CD version. The CD includes an Adobe® PDF file of the lesson plan book and ready-to-use activities or templates that support many of the lessons. Simply copy the files onto your server to make the lessons instantly available to your staff.

Pricing

For each lesson plan book:

School-wide license $199

District-wide license $139* (per school licensed)

* Discounts are available when purchasing multiple titles.

ORDER NOW!

Call 800-877-4292 or your favorite education dealer.

7412 SW Beaverton Hillsdale Hwy, Ste 102
Portland, OR 97225-2167 USA

Phone: 503-297-3004
Fax: 503-297-4676
Email: sales@inspiration.com
www.inspiration.com

Volume licenses available for the following books

- Kidspiration in the Classroom

- Achieving Standards with Inspiration 7

- Inspiration in Language Arts

- Inspiration in Science

(For more information on these books, see page 110)

Inspiration® SOFTWARE, INC

Kidspiration in the Classroom